OUT OF STEP

Pursuing Seamus Heaney to Purgatory

Catherine Byron

*with drawings
by the author*

LOXWOOD STONELEIGH

BRISTOL

First published by Loxwood Stoneleigh 1992

Copyright © 1992 Catherine Byron

Designed and typeset by Falling Wall Press Ltd, Bristol
Printed in Great Britain by Doveton Press Ltd, Bristol
Text printed on recycled paper

Cover design by Darren Seymour

British Library Cataloguing-in-Publication
A catalogue record for this book is available from the British Library

ISBN 1 85135 016 0

Loxwood Stoneleigh
11 Colston Yard, Colston Street, Bristol BS1 5BD, England

For my daughters
Emma and Naomi
who grew up
on this side
of the water

CONTENTS

ILLUSTRATIONS

ACKNOWLEDGEMENTS

Parts of *Out of Step* have appeared, in slightly different form, in the Canadian journal *Brick*, the *Linen Hall Review* and *Sunk Island Review*.

I would like to thank the following authors and publishers for permission to reprint copyright material: Gillian Allnutt for a short passage from *Spitting the Pips Out*; R. Dardis Clarke for four lines from Austin Clarke's poem 'Penal Law'; Sukie Colegrave for a passage from *The Spirit of the Valley*; Faber & Faber Ltd for several quotations from Neil Corcoran's critical study *Seamus Heaney*; Mary Daly for two passages from *Beyond God the Father*; Polly Devlin for a passage from her memoir *All of Us There*; Little, Brown and Company for part of Emily Dickinson's Poem 341; Rutgers University Press for a quotation from 'For the Etruscans: Sexual Difference and Artistic Production – The Debate over a Female Aesthetic' by Rachel Blau Duplessis and members of Workshop 9 in *The Future of Difference*, edited by Hester Eisenstein and Alice Jardine, copyright 1985 by Rutgers, the State University, copyright 1980 by the Barnard College Women's Center; Tim Enright for a passage from his translation of Tomás Ó Crohan's *Island Cross-Talk*; Gwyneth Evans for quotations from E. Estyn Evans' *Irish Folk Ways*; the late John M. Feehan for a passage from his book *Bobby Sands and the Tragedy of Northern Island*; Faber & Faber Ltd for several passages from John Haffenden's *Viewpoints: Poets in Conversation*; Thomas Kinsella for quotations from 'Downstream' and 'Downstream II'; Tavistock Publications for a quotation from R.D. Laing's *The Divided Self*; Edna Longley for passages from her critical study *Poetry in the Wars*; Faber & Faber Ltd for eight lines from Tom Paulin's poem 'The Book of Juniper'; Tim Robinson for a passage from *Stones of Aran*; Carol Rumens for a line from her poem 'The Most Difficult Door'; Margaret Ward for passages from her historical study *Unmanageable Revolutionaries*; Random House Inc. for passages from two works by Alan Watts, *Cloud-Hidden, Whereabouts Unknown* and *Nature, Man and Woman*; and H.A. Williams for a passage from *The True Wilderness*.

Every effort has been made to trace the original copyright holders of works quoted from, but in some instances without success. Loxwood Stoneleigh and I would be glad to be informed of any such omission, so that it could be rectified in any future edition of this book.

I owe special thanks to Faber & Faber Ltd for permission to quote extensively from the works of Seamus Heaney; to Rev. Richard Mohan, Prior of Saint Patrick's Purgatory, Lough Derg, for permission to reproduce the Order of the Station as an Appendix; and to the Suirbheireacht Ordonais in Dublin for the use of maps as the basis of some of my illustrations. Seamus Heaney kindly answered some specific queries about the first poem in his sequence 'Station Island', and about 'Triptych III' in his collection *Fieldwork*.

I would like to thank family and friends in Ireland whose warm hospitality made my travels so much easier, and friends and colleagues there and elsewhere whose conversations and letters illuminated and encouraged me. In particular, I am indebted to my parents, Peggy and David Greenfield, and to Kristine Beuret, Eileen Coxon, Paul Durcan, Michael Farley, Laurence J. Flynn, Anne Le Marquand Hartigan, Janice Kulyk Keefer, Medbh McGuckian, Carole Satyamurti and the late Norah Shovlin.

Finally, I am most grateful to the Leverhulme Foundation for a Research Award which made it possible for me to forgo freelance work for several months while I completed this book, and for an earlier East Midlands Arts major bursary which financed travel to Ireland.

Catherine Byron
Leicester, July 1992

PART ONE

On the Way to the Island

CHAPTER ONE

Light-headed, Leaving Home

Sunday 2 August 1987: 10 a.m.
    At the bus station

> ... you must go inland and be
> Lost in compassion's ecstasy,
> Where suffering soars in summer air –

> Patrick Kavanagh, 'Prelude'

The journey from Dublin to Lough Derg

Donegal – Dun na nGall – literally the fort of the foreigner, but in reality the most intact and beautiful of the counties of Ireland's western seaboard. It lies almost surrounded by 'the foreigner'; its inland border is *that* Border, its eastern farmlands are the lost hinterland of Derry City. To reach it from the Republic, you must either travel across the triangle of British territory that presses west right along the great waterways of Lough Erne, or go to Sligo Town and hug a narrow strip of coast northwards until the massive promontory of Glencolumbcille promises the Atlantic and the mountainous extent of this, Ireland's northernmost, but not Northern, county.

I am a foreigner there myself, half-English and half-Galway by blood, Belfast by raising; but Donegal is my country of the mind, and the physical country to which I keep returning from various and ever-changing exiles. It is the source-book of my identity, both as woman and as writer. Long-lapsed from the religious faith of my childhood, I come to Donegal for my own, usually solitary, retreats, and the land itself is my spiritual director – along, of course, with the ocean. As Alan Watts says of the motion of another ocean, the Pacific: 'It harmonizes with our very breathing. It does not count our days.'[1]

Today I am taking a bus up to Donegal from Dublin City, but on this occasion I am not going to the Atlantic, nor even to the mountains. The service is circumscribed: this is the Lough Derg run. It will take me, not to Donegal Town, nor to the intricate and cliffed coast to the north, but to a dead-end hidden away in the southern inland hills: Catholic pilgrims are the only regular visitors from the outside world to this border country of small farms and army patrols. Lough Derg is not on the way to anywhere but itself.

I have been there before, but in mid-winter. I have never seen it during the pilgrimage season when, from the first of June to the fifteenth of August, nearly thirty thousand people still come to the ferry house each year, and buy a great coin of a token to give to the boatman who will speed them over the bare half mile of sullen water to Saint Patrick's Purgatory. For it is to this most ancient and most rigorous of penitential pilgrimages that I am setting out, on Ireland's Bank Holiday Monday. I go with the blessing of my favourite uncle and aunt, who fell in love nearly forty years ago on this very pilgrimage. Their daughter has just dropped me down to Bus Aras. With me will travel those two young girls – sisters? – with their noses deep in a Mills and Boon apiece, this middle-aged man in the comfortable tweeds, the young fellow over by the ticket office who could be a rugger hero. Surely not the overweight woman in that fluttery pink silk dress and matching jacket, and four-inch heels? Yes, the bus's departure has been announced on the tannoy, and she has joined the queue with the rest of us.

We board the bus, and the inspector comes aboard for a quick word with us all. Had we seen the programme on Telefis Eireann last night about the chief Irish pilgrimages – Croagh Patrick, Knock, and Saint Patrick's Purgatory? And would we all squeeze in a wee prayer for him when we were on Lough Derg? He waves us off with respect and good humour. I savour the moment. In Ireland it is possible still to feel part of an unbroken order, a culture in which certain common assumptions are held about the spiritual side of life. To me, a child of the divided North, and then a longtime dweller in cynical and pluralist England, this brings an unaccustomed sense of belonging. There is a classlessness here that delights me. I know too well that Ireland since independence has been stifled socially and politically by the closeness of Church and State, but the *lingua franca* of a common faith, whatever that faith's deficiencies, creates a commonwealth of acceptance I luxuriate in. Temporarily.

As the bus carries us out of Dublin's undistinguished suburbs on the road to Kells and Cavan, I feel less attached to my fellow-passengers. This road usually takes me to the wild places, to the sea coasts, and the mountains that hang over them, out in the north-west. I feel cross and cheated.

Why spend three days crowded on to a tiny freshwater island with hundreds of others when I could be alone in the wilderness? I remember wryly other words of Alan Watts, about the indoor nature of Christianity, 'the closed sanctuary where the light of the open sky comes only through the symbolic jewelry of stained-glass windows ... Looking at trees and rocks, at the sky with its clouds or stars, at the sea, or at a naked human body, I find myself in a world where this religion simply does not fit ... the Christian world, as we know it, is only a half-world in which the feeling and the symbolically feminine is unassimilated.'[2]

The unassimilated feminine – ah, that is the very thing that has sent me on this odd quest. I have been caught up in a momentum of questions about spirituality and poetry and the feminine by my reading of Seamus Heaney's sequence 'Station Island', twelve poems that loosely follow the shape and time sequence of the three-day pilgrimage at Saint Patrick's Purgatory. The most urgent of those questions is: how is it that, in a poem that is almost entirely peopled by male characters (there are female presences, but they are notably silent and unnamed), I get so strong a sense of the feminine? I know from Heaney's earlier work, and from what he has said about the process of writing, that his poetry is unusual (for an Irish male poet) in its conscious drawing on the male and the female: 'The process [of finding poems] is a kind of somnambulist encounter between masculine will and intelligence and feminine clusters of image and emotion.'[3] In 'Station Island' there is a great deal of literal somnambulism – it is almost a dream-vision poem in the medieval tradition – but it challenges me as none of Heaney's previous works has done to tease out the complexities of those 'feminine clusters'.

There is so slender an inheritance of poetry written by women in Ireland. As reader, and as poet, I have to look to male forerunners in Irish writing more than I do in English, or Scottish, or Welsh – let alone North American. And, amongst the Irish male poets, I have found Heaney the

most articulate and transparent witness to the conflicting
pulls of art and gender. But what is going on in *this* poem?
The worrying voyeurism of the 'bog poems' of *North* (1975)
had been to a great extent absorbed and exorcised in the
celebratory and painful poems of married love in *Fieldwork*
(1979). Now, five years later, this sequence, centred in a
collection that bears its name, opens a new and difficult
round in the poet's 'encounter'.

As I read and reread the poems with this question
nagging at me, other questions arise. Why has Heaney set
a sequence that amounts to a poetic autobiography within
what he has Joyce deride as 'your peasant pilgrimage',[4] a
devotional exercise at the heart of the unregenerate
patriarchy of Irish Catholicism? Why choose a pilgrimage
held amidst the still fresh waters of a lake, when the
hallowed Irish tradition of *peregrinatio*[5] sets the spirit afloat
on the boundless salt waves of ocean: oarless, but in God's
hands? Why all this emphasis on circling, on treading the
same place sunwise? Where is Sweeney in all this, the wild
and recusant madman, the tinker, the outsider escaped as
a bird into restlessness and non-responsibility? His spirit
hovers both in the translation of the medieval text *Buile
Suibhne* that Heaney published around the same time, and
in the section of poems that follows 'Station Island' in the
collection *Station Island*, called 'Sweeney Redivivus'. And
finally, why is there no guide, no sibyl or even Virgil-
figure, to take the poet down into the world of the untimely
dead?

I have been reading and researching for months, and
have discovered much about the history and prehistory of
the Purgatory that may offer partial answers to some of
these questions. But now I have started on my own
pilgrimage: I have been fasting since midnight, and I will
not have a bed to lie in until the night after this one, for I
will be on vigil. The uneven roads of Ireland's boggy
midlands buffet me, but I try to doze. I think of Dante's
dark wood, Langland's 'felde ful of folke'.

> I was a fasted pilgrim,
> light-headed, leaving home
> to face into my station.
>
> Poem I

*   *   *

I jerk awake as our bus reaches the Border. A new traffic light system has been installed since I was here in January – half-roadblocks and sharp ramps. We wait for half an hour in a painfully slow queue to be allowed into County Fermanagh. The dark shadow of Heaney's ninth poem falls on me from the camouflaged watchtower of the British army post: what does my three-day fast have to do with the pain and wasting of the hunger-striker Francis Hughes' death after fifty-nine days without food? What does poetry, or mysticism, or penitence, have to offer in the way of answers to that extremity?

Heaney speaks of the 'complex pieties ... implicit in the very terrain I was born in.'[6] Those pieties involve areas of politics and of feminine and masculine tendency and allegiance that I feel I have only begun to fathom. As we near the village of Pettigo, and enter the ancient *termon* – or sanctuary land – that surrounds Lough Derg, I begin to re-enter the terrain of my own past. Although pilgrims come from all Ireland, 'doing one's station' is and always has been most popular amongst the Catholics of the North. Memories stir of guns thrust at the car window when I was a child, of the unquiet ghost of my own murdered uncle.[7] I will carry my own nightmares with me on to Station Island, as I will take my own self-accusation of defensiveness[8] and of too-quiet acceptances:

> '... I hate how quick I was to know my place.
> I hate where I was born, hate everything
> That made me biddable and unforthcoming, ...'
>
> Poem IX

NOTES

1. *Cloud-Hidden, Whereabouts Unknown: A Mountain Journal*, p.11.
2. *Nature, Man and Woman*, pp.26-8.
3. *Preoccupations*, p.34.
4. 'Station Island' XII.
5. Irish monks of the Middle Ages were famous for their willingness to abandon themselves to the ocean and God's will in their skin boats. The *Anglo-Saxon Chronicle* records the arrival of a small party at King Alfred's court in Wessex: they had set off without any steering gear or oars, to make landfall wherever God willed. Saint Brendan the Navigator and his companions are perhaps the most famous, and their wanderings have in recent years been reconstructed by a modern-day *peregrinus*-cum-explorer, Tim Severin, and recorded in his *The Brendan Voyage*.
6. *Preoccupatons*, p.35.
7. The uncle was in fact an uncle by marriage, a 'real' uncle's brother-in-law; in terms of the Irish valuing of the extended family, and of his living near us, he was closer than many of my blood-uncles.
8. See William Carleton's words to the pilgrim Heaney in Poem II:

> ... though there's something natural in your smile
> there's something in it strikes me as defensive.

CHAPTER TWO

At the Water's Edge

January 1987: Three islands –
Iniskeel, Station Island, and Boa.

'The tides parted and I crossed
barefoot to Inishkeel.

Where was the lost crozier
among the scorched bracken?

And where was that freshet
of sweet water?

Goosegrass and broken walls
were all my sanctuary ...'

Tom Paulin, 'The Book of Juniper'

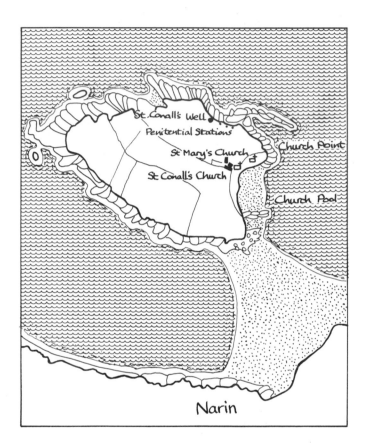

Iniskeel

January the fifth of the same year. Michael and I are in West Donegal, in a cottage at the sea's edge. It is a sort of late honeymoon, only the second time in our year together that we have been able to get away on our own for more than a night. And to Ireland!

All evening, on the drive here through the mountains, the rain has beaten down and against us. In the morning we find that the sea has reluctantly drawn back from the very door of our cottage in the night. Great piles of oarweed have been raked from the lower shore and dumped right up to the step. The whole pale strand of Narin is looped and heaped with this heavy harvest, and a band of rooks is ransacking it for pickings alongside the gulls, a raucous alternation of black and startling white set against the weed's rich oranges and browns.

The storm has cleared the sky utterly, and for days we are to have bright, hard weather: a low golden sun, for the solstice is scarcely a fortnight gone; frosts so unusually hard for this western seaboard that even the runnels of fresh water cutting through salt sand to the sea freeze in their courses. Some mornings, there is a hoary bloom on the stranded fronds of the oarweed, until the sun re-gilds it.

I am showing Donegal to Michael, who has never before been this far north in Ireland. It is, after all, the recipient of many love poems in my work, so it is only fair to introduce it to him. Our days, then, while the brief light lasts, are visitations to places many-layered in memories for me, but revelations for him – the great white strand of Maghera under the cliffs of the Glencolumbcille peninsula; Loughros Mor where the *Duquesa Santa Ana* foundered in 1588, running hopelessly for Spain; the old rabbit warren in the dunes of Cashelgolan; Gweebarra Bay and Trawenagh Bay.

One place is in our eye morning and evening, framing our day's journeying – the island of Iniskeel. It lies in the arms of Narin's bay, but its interest arises from more than its constant presence: it is one of those islands that the phases of the moon grant access to. For days on each side of the full moon a sand causeway appears at the ebb tide, and the island is open to visitor and farmer alike. Cattle are led over for their summer grazing, birdwatchers go in search of the rare terns that nest there, fishers for the excellent shore-fishing on its seaward side. For Tom Paulin it is the only place in which he can dream of the successful and peaceful establishment of 'that sweet equal republic' vainly fought for in Ireland's 1798.[1]

For myself, I have long since renounced my childhood delight in hooking Iniskeel's fine edible crabs from their hiding-places with a rusty golf-club. Now it is the strange gift of its accessibility, its moon-held periodicity, that draws me to it,[2] and the patterns of visitation and ritual that this accessibility made possible in the past.

For from early Christian times Iniskeel has been the centre and starting point of a pilgrimage that is still undertaken, unostentatiously, by local people. I remember walking through the grey ruins of the church and monastery of Saint Conall when it was dunged by the summer cattle, and leant over by knapweed and yellow flaggers. They stood – and stand still – in a gapped enclosure of ancient and recent graves in the lee of the island, above the landward bay of Church Pool. Now, in winter light, and seen over unwadable winter seas, the ruins seem paler and cleaner, but are hard to make out. I want to walk their ground again now, in winter, as the generations of summer pilgrims have down the centuries.

Beyond the ruined monastic buildings and the ancient graveyard crosses are the penitential Stations of Iniskeel. The island itself is the first 'station' in a prescribed journey or *turas* that takes in other holy sites – wells and crosses – in the locality, a distance in all of over twenty miles. To fulfil the *turas*'s requirements these days it is sufficient to visit Iniskeel only, and some pilgrims even use cars to drive across the causeway when the moon is at its fullest. But some aspects of the devotion are as they always were: the penitential season still begins on Saint Conall's feastday, the twentieth of May, and continues until the twelfth of September.

On the island's northern shore, facing the greater island of Aranmor, and scolded in the early part of the season by nesting terns, the pilgrim lies first of all on the stone slab that is Saint Conall's Bed, then rises and takes water from the holy well. The penitential stations themselves are three piles of stones, and the pilgrim must walk round each of them fifteen times in prayer, throwing a stone on to the pile after each round. The last task is to say fifteen decades of the rosary while walking (sunwise of course) round the ruined churches of Saint Conall and Saint Mary. The whole 'station' is still a normal part of the lives of friends, some younger than me, who live there.

Station – the word keeps recurring, as things mysteriously do when one is alert to them. I had known the Catholic devotion of the 'Stations of the Cross' from childhood, never querying the word which elsewhere in my world meant a place for tickets and trains. Since reading *Station Island*, the word has acquired hooks of the sort that atoms are said to have, and draws other meanings to it to create a compound of ever-increasing complexity.

Whilst reading the Blasket islander Tomás Ó Crohan's *Island Cross-Talk*, I had come across this (complete) diary entry for April 1921:

The Day of the 'Station'

It is 'Station' day for us. God's messengers have come to visit us. The parish priest left instructions at Dunquin on Sunday that they should be fetched on Monday if it was fine. If not, on the Tuesday. But Monday was glorious on sea and land.

The islanders were washed and in their Sunday best to meet them. You would think they had never known a poor day. The priests were pleased with them, and they were pleased with each other. The priests were in the island by seven o'clock in the morning. Two masses were said and since they had the fine day to spend as they pleased, they were in no

great hurry to leave. They bring their own luncheon
and all the islanders have to do is prepare it. The
parish priest intends having a month's holiday with us
before long.

When they were standing outside on the green near
the main road, with the sun shining brightly above
their heads, the priests declared that the island was a
wonderful place.[3]

In a note, Ó Crohan's translator Tim Enright explains that
'station' can also mean a Mass brought to the places where
ordinary people live, such as a private house. On the Great
Blasket, which had no resident priest or church of its own,
the islanders could hear Mass only rarely, in their
schoolhouse, at the unpredictable convenience of the
mainland priests and, of course, the sea.

Looking across at Iniskeel, inaccessible only by a matter
of tens of yards, I ponder this reversal. Here, and on
countless places round Ireland's coasts and lake shores, it
is the lay people who go to the island in pilgrimage, for the
islands are the places apart where the saints sought solitude
and simplicity of life, where they built beehive cells and
small oratories that are still traceable in the stony fields.
The people must cross over to 'do their station'. But in the
case of the Blasket islanders, 'God's messengers' carried the
rite of the Mass over with them in a curragh, along with
the materials for their luncheon.

Station, from the Latin *statio* – a post of duty, a picket; a
fixed place, an anchorage; a standing still. Does it mean
both a duty, then, and a time for stillness, in the context of
these Irish observances? Iniskeel is not yet ready to admit
us dryshod to its hallowed ground. And another island,
named with this very name of 'station', must also be
studied, at a distance and from the shore, before the week
is up and we have to drive east to Belfast.

Station Island, after all, has been a major excuse for this
week's visit to the west. We expect it will be deserted – no
pilgrims, and presumably no clergy there either, not in

January. The season could not be further from the green summer months of the pilgrimage, the 'tender, bladed growth' of Poem I. Our interest on this occasion is topographical: we want to photograph what we can of the island in its setting in order to illustrate a talk I am giving the following month. Will we learn anything about Station Island over and above the images we frame in the lens of the camera?

Years of living in England's Midlands have made me forget how short are the hours of daylight at these northern latitudes so soon after the winter solstice. But the unusual winter clarity of hard frost and cloudless skies is laying the gilded distances of Donegal before us in ways unimaginable in the 'soft' weather so frequent in an Irish summer. Mount Errigal's quartzite cone in the northern highlands of the county glitters on our skyline, holding out an earnest of that clarity in Donegal's interior as well as on the coast. The conditions are ideal for the photography.

Why then do we put off going to Lough Derg until the last day possible?

*   *   *

January the tenth. We have driven over from the coast, south and inland. The hills become low and undistinguished as we leave the Blue Stack Mountains and head cross-country on the minor road from Laghy, just south of Donegal Town. By using the Laghy road direct to Pettigo, instead of the main roads a few miles further south, we can avoid crossing into the North at Belleek and then back into the Republic twelve miles later at Pettigo itself. Suddenly the Border forces itself on our attention and affects our movements. Pettigo is one of the 'approved' crossings.

The name is derived from another Latin word, *protectio*, itself a translation in this context of the Gaelic word for sanctuary, *termon*. But there is little at first sight to set

Pettigo apart from any other small town in Ireland, except
the uneasy trappings of its border status: Irish customs post
this side of the River Termon, and, over the stone bridge,
the Brits in evidence – sandbagged lookouts, camouflage
colours.

Staying on the Donegal – and Republican – side, we hug
the western bank of the small river and follow its course up
out of the grey village, through the scatter of the hamlet of
Carn, and then on, along a road like any other in the west's
undramatic interior. It bucks and slithers with the
undulations of the bog under its tarmac. Ancient roads of
timber are still found buried in Irish bogs, *toghers* that ride
the waterlogged ground like a lithe raft, mile after mile.
Was there one here, centuries ago, when this was a
highroad famous throughout Europe? When the road to
Lough Derg was the way that led to an entrance to the
Underworld as famous as Avernus?

Reading about Station Island in the libraries of England
has filled me with visions and old stories: myths, medieval
'best-sellers', accounts of initiations. As we pass a sign
saying 'Lough Derg 5' by a rushy field, I am impatient to
know how the place will fit with these images born of
books. Can this really be a place that was part of Dante's
received wisdom on the Underworld? The ground rises,
and the road seems to head into nowhere.

The pelt of the hills around us now is sphagnum and
sedge, except for the black-green geometry of spruce
plantations, and the dark lines where turf has been freshly
cut. There is nothing much to suggest that, over a rise, past
a tiny flagstone quarry, the lough will start to reveal itself.
And when it appears, it is not the mere cyclops eye of a
tarn, but the first silver corner of a great islanded expanse
of clear, cold water set in the saucered hills. It is Lough
Derg.

And the islands? And Station Island? We scan the
complex arms and bays of bright water, and find that, in
contrast to the blanket bog and serried plantations of the
shore, they are naturally wooded. In the golden January

light the alders on them are damson-coloured, the willows aflame. Scots pine and juniper anchor them down on the water with the dark weight of their greenness. One of them, almost out of sight to the north, must be Saint's Island, and on it the monastery ruins have long since been reclaimed by the wild wood.[4] But our eyes are drawn inevitably to the island that is as different as possible from the rest – Station Island. Its grey and verdigris solidity, its high-rise masonry, are built four-square in the midst of wilderness and water.

Entrance to the Underworld? Place of penitence and meditation? To our eyes, straining from the shore, it looks more like a place of long-term incarceration, the prison island of Alcatraz. And a construction company with heavy plant on the shore and on the island, and with great barges plying between, is busy erecting a many-storeyed new building on the west side of the already impossibly crowded fastness. We watch an all-male bunch of managers, overweight in their sheepskin jackets, speed back from the site in a launch, and then off up the road in a fast car. The island they leave in their wake looks unutterably grim.

How on earth does all *this* fit with the romance and sensationalism of my reading? For the history of Saint Patrick's Purgatory and of the lake it is set in has taken me into areas of legend and speculation that I had not expected.

*   *   *

The first story is a naming myth, a circuitous account of the meaning of the *dearg* in Lough Derg. Finn Mac Cool was an Ulster giant, the layer-down of the pillared basalt of the Giant's Causeway, trickster, champion (and figurehead this year of a new publicity campaign by the Northern Ireland Tourist Board). I had read that it was his scatterbrained son Conan who was the doubtful hero of the naming of Lough Derg.

Ignoring sage warnings, Conan carelessly tossed the old thigh bone of a witch into the lough. A worm concealed in it was freed, and, like a horsehair worm in its need for water, drew nourishment from its splashdown, and grew into a monster ready to devour the whole of Ireland. For a time this monster was prepared to get by on a mere two hundred cattle a day. Conan, fast acquiring both courage and discretion, disguised himself in a cow-skin, and was eaten, along with a hundred and ninety-nine cows, on the summit of Crocknacunny Mountain. (With the aid of the Ordnance Survey map, and feeling rather silly, I identify this as a slight elevation on the eastern shore of the lough. Can one mix myth and hard geography?) In the evil heat of the monster's innards every hair of Conan's body was stripped away; then, in a shocking birth to follow this monstrous mockery of death, he hacked his way out through the hitherto invulnerable hide, and in doing so fatally wounded the unwillingly pregnant monster.

It is at this point that the saintly intervention occurs, as it does so often in such tales of early Ireland. The timing of the event had fortuitously coincided with the period of Christianity's coming, and Saint Patrick arrived to give the *coup de grâce*. With the superior strength of the new religion, he pinned the great corpse to the bottom of the lough, and so it was that the waters were stained red with the monster's blood, and it was named *Loch Dearg*, the red lake. You can still see the fossilised bones of the creature exposed to the air when the level is low . . .

In this earliest story, the themes of many of the rest announce themselves: a death that is chosen, and a painful resurrection; a pagan beginning with a Christian continuation; a naming; and, at the heart of the adventure, a stripping down to bald identity. Over the centuries these themes grow and shift, but are hardly changed in their concern with death, purging and a sort of second life.

Some recent authorities have preferred a different etymology, deriving Derg from *deirc*, the Irish for cave, and so centring attention on the historically attested rites on

Station Island rather than on picturesque myth. But for the moment I am not concerned to weigh the merits of the rival explanations. There seems to me to be something more important *not* going on here.

I worry about Conan. Did he really need to go to such lengths in order to be 'reborn'? Does female power and fertility have to be so mocked, and (deep insult to Ireland, country of cattle since time immemorial!) in the context of cattle-raising? Elsewhere in Irish legend the pre- and post-Christian ways of seeing have melded to give us the goddess-saint Brigid, guardian of cattle and dairying. In the parishes of rural Ireland holy wells and springs, sacred now to the saints, preserve the ancient worship of water. But in relation to this place, this holiest of Ireland's ancient shrines, the stories seem strangely one-sided.

No matter how far back I trace the records, I can find no hint of another mode of relating to stone and water here at Lough Derg, only this violence, and a succession of spiritual and territorial take-over bids. I consider the suggestion in one legend that Saint Patrick's first rôle here was to oust the druids from Station Island: does this alternative to the Conan version, the one in which the witch-born monster dies in a travesty of childbirth, contain a clue to that exclusion of the feminine that bothers me in this place and its history? I think of Tacitus's graphic account of the women and men of Anglesey, fighting side by side to resist the coming of the Romans to that druid stronghold. The druids were the shaman-priests of Celtic culture, which was

> ... perhaps the last great mystical culture and religion of Europe, with roots going back to a prehistoric love of earth and water, trees and stars, and worship of the cosmic Mother. It was a religion of myth and legend, told and retold, forbidden to be written down ...[5]

Station Island is in the pocket of my coat as we walk down to the deserted pier by the ferry house. Somehow it

seems irrelevant now to take it out. After all, Heaney in his
'Station Island' sequence has not concerned himself with
these prehistories, or even with the histories of the island's
medieval fame as an entrance to the Underworld. He meets
ghosts, yes, but not in that formal and structured way. Yet
Heaney is a master of *absences* in his poetry, and an image
comes to me from Poem III:

> I thought of walking round
> and round a space utterly empty,
> utterly a source, like the idea of sound; ...

These are the words of a poet who is himself in deep
sympathy with the idea of the unwritten and the
unwritable, and perhaps with that literal *tact* of the druids.
I know that what is omitted from Heaney's poem is likely
to be as significant for my understanding of it as what is in
it. Somehow, in ways I cannot yet articulate, he has
included by their palpable absence the possibility of these
very questions being raised.

Station Island itself eludes us. The intense frost that has
given us the gold of a low sun has iced the pier
treacherously. The verdigris dome of the basilica rises
above a conglomeration of buildings that mean nothing to
us, and we turn back to follow the shore round to the west.
This too is no wild and lonely venture: all is 'bleared,
smeared with toil; / And wears man's smudge and shares
man's smell'.[6] As we move away from the noises of cranes
and cement-mixers, the whine of chain-saws gashes the
returning silence. The Irish Forestry Commission is in
action, and we walk through a whole hillside of harvested
sitka spruce.

We are hopelessly at odds with one another. Going
down to the lower shore to avoid the logging work, we are
still, uncharacteristically, arguing and caught out of kilter
in some distress we cannot understand. We glimpse Station
Island from time to time through stands of forest that are
still intact. I feel defensive about it; hold no brief, after all

these years, for the institutions of Catholicism, but am not prepared to be so utterly repelled as Michael by the sight of those grim facades. If we are both agnostics, both post-Christians who see spirituality in a wider philosophical context – why are we arguing so bitterly from the corners of the Roman and Anglican sects we have left behind? I walk off alone and stand looking down into the rocky shallows at the edge of the water, haunted by the horrible image in Heaney's anguished Poem IX – of the strange polyp 'surreal as a shed breast' floating down the 'mucky, glittering flood'.

We walk back to the car, slowly putting ourselves together. The loggers are grappling the cleaned trunks on to a transporter now, and there is a scent of unfired incense in the air. Resin oozings from the stumps are frozen to amber beads; the stumps themselves, and the coarse chippings of the saw, are furred with hoar frost. We find astonishing pinks and reds round the just-severed heartwood. And we suddenly decide to drive the few miles south to the softer land- and waterscape of Lough Erne. Can it be that the very atmosphere of Lough Derg – whether blood red lake, or lake of the cave – is the cause of our quarrel? We will go to another ancient site of which Heaney has written, and see what happens to our tempers there!

Back at Pettigo we ask at the Irish Customs Post about Boa Island. Can they tell us where to look for the famous Janus-faced stones? The young official gets out a large-scale map, but cannot help. He has never heard of what we are after, and doesn't know that stretch of country. It is, after all, British territory, even though it is only two miles to the south of where we are standing. For Pettigo is not just ancient sanctuary land, nor is it just a modern border post. The twelve miles between it and the small town of Belleek to the west enclose a 'salient' of the North, a little sliver of lake shore that is Fermanagh's. Its position, as one of the two points at which Donegal – and so the Border – touches the shores of Lough Erne, made it a centre of dispute and tension in 1922, and at times thereafter.

Part of that salient, too, is Boa Island, named long ago for Badhbh, the ancient goddess of war, and now a somnolent stretched spine scarcely raised from the lake waters. It carries the smart A47 (the quality of the road surface being a useful reminder of which side of the Border you are on in this part of Ireland) along its two and a half miles, hardly giving away its island status by the two short and discreet bridges at each end.

And so we cross the bridge into Fermanagh, and drive to the bridge across the Rannagh River. Soon after, we can double back and drive west again, this time along the spine of Boa. Surely there will be a sign there to direct us to the famous stone heads?

*   *   *

It is the third section of the sequence 'Triptych' in *Fieldwork* that has brought us here; and my long memories, too, of strange images in books about ancient Ireland: the cult of the severed head, the glad eye of the *sheila-na-gig*, the solemnity of the early saints in effigy. Heaney's 'god-eyed, sex-mouthed stone' and his 'carved monastic heads ... crumbling like bread on water' have called us south to this softer, more intricate lake, fringed with *phragmites* and interlaced with waterways. The mountains are visible as a backdrop, but this is a lowland lough, with much to remind one of Ulster's (and Ireland's) greatest stretch of fresh water, the linked loughs, Neagh and Beg – whose flat inland littoral was Heaney's first home.

We have no further luck with our enquiries. In Ireland the old sites, even those pictured in book after book on Irish art and archaeology, are often quite invisible to the casual visitor. I remember tracking down the Turoe Stone, one of the most glorious examples of La Tène art, in a cowfield at the end of a boreen deep in east Galway, not ten miles from my mother's family farm. There *was* a signpost, if you knew you were looking for one; and in the end, if you were patient, the stone, small though it was, made its own summons across pathless pasture. The old woman in the nearby farmhouse nearly missed her chance to sell me a blurred black and white postcard of it – the only gesture towards commercialism and catering for the tourist in her guardianship of the treasure on her family's land.

It is no surprise, then, that on deserted midwinter Boa we can find no clue along the only road that traverses it. The verse in Heaney's poem gives no co-ordinates of that sort:

> On Boa the god-eyed, sex-mouthed stone
> Socketed between graves, two-faced, trepanned,
> Answered my silence with silence.
> A stoup for rain water. Anathema.

The famous heads elude us, and the winter sun is already making absurd shadows. We give up easily, and drive on west to the British checkpoint. There is a hold-up there, because an escaped IRA prisoner is on the run and suspected of being in the area. Then a mile or two later a contingent of the Irish Army stops us and scrutinises Michael's beard suspiciously. After a careful examination of his documents, we are allowed on into Donegal, and try to forget about the Border for a time.

But we find ourselves talking of how shadowed Heaney's poem is with Border tensions; how, like us on this road, he has to listen to 'the thick rotations / Of an army helicopter patrolling'. And of how those islands of Erne hold their own counsel. We cannot let the poem alone. Devenish, Boa, Horse Island – from verse to verse they offer a progress from crumbling Christian monument to pagan silence to deserted hearthstone. All the man hears and does not hear, all that he sees, makes him want 'to bow down, to offer up, / To go barefoot, foetal and penitential,

/ And pray at the water's edge.'

That injunction reverberates from my childhood: *Offer it up* – the long-since shrugged-off answer to all the promptings of self, a *via negativa* that sweetened too many years of submission and self-denial. And here is Heaney suggesting a possibility of return to those conditioned responses! It is not until months later, when I am on Station Island as a pilgrim, that I will realise the full force of this poem's title – 'At the Water's Edge'. Here, skirting this edge of Lough Erne along to Ballyshannon and the sea, I feel rebellious and unsatisfied. I dismiss the line that follows:

How we crept before we walked!

with its suggestion of the need to go back into the understandings of childhood, of the need to remake one's own making. I try to stop thinking of the other painful and bloody birthings – for Ulster and for Ireland – alluded to in the poem's concluding lines:

I remembered
The helicopter shadowing our march at Newry,
The scared, irrevocable steps.

Heaney is remembering the huge protest march in Newry in February 1972, the Sunday after Derry's Bloody Sunday, when the helicopters blared over the heads of the crowd, 'You are breaking the law. You are breaking the law.'[7] In those marred months I was suckling my first child in England's soft and astonishingly undisturbed south. I was not a witness, but an artless and speechless long-distance voyeur. My guilt at that emotional and geographical dislocation from the events in my old country, at that solipsistic absorption in motherhood, troubles me anew. My temper has not improved.

I am impatient with all this foot-bound emphasis on steps and walking, whether on the Erne islands or on

Station Island. Heaney, surely, is a poet who both 'recreates the exhilaration of meditative solitary driving',[8] and is 'up and away' in the bird-guise of Sweeney. Wheels and wings are, for the moment, modes of transport that I incline to also.

So we head west, eager for the sharp salt airs of the Atlantic, and then over the mountains towards Gweebarra and 'home'. Great banks of freezing fog ride out west round the foothills of Crownarad and Cracknapeast, but the road through the pass is almost clear. That night, I put my copy of *Station Island* to one side, and start, with a lightening of the heart, to re-read Heaney's translation of *Sweeney Astray*. I hunger for the flights of a tale that takes all Ireland into its restless range.

NOTES

1. See 'The Book of Juniper' in *Liberty Tree*.
2. See Tim Robinson's excellent essay, *Walking out to Islands*.
3. *Island Cross-Talk*, p.122. Some months later I mentioned this Blasket Island 'station' to my mother, and she told me that it was a regular custom during her childhood in East Galway for Mass to be said in the houses of the parishioners. It was a special event that came around to each farmhouse about once in four years, and the whole house and yard were given a great spring-clean: all the neighbours came to hear Mass, which was said in the kitchen, and sat down to a feast afterwards. In her townland of Ballinahistle there were two holdings: her house was traditionally visited near Christmas, and the neighbours' house at Eastertime.
4. See *Lough Derg* by Alice Curtayne, pp.19-22.
5. Anne Bancroft, *Origins of the Sacred*, p.87.
6. Gerard Manley Hopkins, 'God's Grandeur'.
7. From Seamus Heaney's own account of this incident, in a letter to the author.
8. Neil Corcoran, *Seamus Heaney*, p.65.

CHAPTER THREE

Sweeney Astray

Buile Suibhne and Poem I

January 1987: Donegal to Belfast

> Sometimes naked, sometimes mad,
> Now as a scholar, now as a fool,
> Thus they appear on earth –
> The free men!
>
> Hindu proverb

A 'Saint Patrick's Step' near the monastery of Clonmacnoise

'**O**ne way or another, he seemed to have been with me from the start': with these words Heaney introduces Sweeney at the start of his translation of the medieval text *Buile Suibhne*. He had published it in Ireland in 1983, the year before *Station Island* came out, and in England in 1984, to coincide with it. And sure enough, there Sweeney is at the start of the 'Station Island' sequence, in the shape of Simon Sweeney – tinker, hedger, haunter of childhood bedrooms:

> 'I was your mystery man
> and am again this morning. ...'

But this latter-day Sweeney is also a dead Sweeney, the first ghost of the succession of unquiet ghosts that Heaney will have to deal with in the sequence – 'old Sabbath-breaker / who has been dead for years'. His voice from the grave, though, falls on unwilling ears. The warning he shouts, to stay clear of all processions, is ignored by Heaney's light-headed pilgrim persona. Why? Who and what precisely is Heaney banishing from the poem? I know that I need to re-acquaint myself with the first Sweeney, to go back past Heaney's own Sweeney poems, and past Flann O'Brien's funny and melancholy Sweeney in *At Swim Two Birds* – and was it just Sweeney *Todd* that T.S. Eliot had in mind? Hush. I read on into *Sweeney Astray*.

Our summer cottage feels as chill on this sub-zero evening as the original Sweeney's cold lairs on the hills of Ireland. Shivering over a smoky coal fire I stop worrying about the way Heaney the pilgrim turns away from 'Simon Sweeney' in Poem I of 'Station Island' when he chooses instead the 'drugged path' to Lough Derg. For I am caught up again in the ancient story of Sweeney the king, a tale in prose and verse that greens and buds in Heaney's vivid translation. The 'hurry of bell-notes', which quickens the pilgrim's step on the road to Purgatory's island, now fades. I hear instead the contentious, territorial chink of Ronan the cleric's bell in 637 AD, as the zealous missionary marks out the site for a church in the midst of Sweeney's kingdom. This is the beginning of the contest that will turn the powerful pagan ruler into a vagrant and a bird, and drive him out of his wits. His response to the challenge is swift:

> Sweeney was suddenly angered and rushed away to hunt the cleric from the church. Eorann, his wife, a daughter of Conn of Ciannacht, tried to hold him back and snatched at the fringe of his crimson cloak, but the silver cloak-fastener broke at the shoulder and sprang across the room. She got the cloak all right but Sweeney had bolted, stark naked, and soon landed with Ronan.
>
> He found the cleric glorifying the King of heaven and earth, in full voice in front of his psalter, a beautiful illuminated book. Sweeney grabbed the book and flung it into the cold depths of a lake nearby, where it sank without trace. Then he took hold of Ronan ...[1]

Now *there's* a proper use for a lake! What a *non serviam*, I think, feeling more than usually anti-clerical – which is, of course, a time-honoured way to feel in a Catholic country. Even the miraculous restoration of the arrogant cleric's psalter in the next paragraph does not dismay me. It is, after all, a pleasing picture, and reminiscent of the world of early Irish nature poetry, with its suggestion of the harmony between humans and animals: the otter rising out of the lake and bringing the precious book to its owner, unmarked in spite of its day and night under water. Never mind for the moment that its recipient will be implacable towards the naked and hot-tempered Sweeney. This is, after all, a key moment in the spiritual history of Ireland. The conflict between Ronan and Sweeney is close to the knuckle for both of them.

For *Sweeney Astray* is a story that focuses on the tragic, radiant, moment of Christianity's arrival amongst a puzzled and passionate people – 'the newly dominant Christian ethos and the older, recalcitrant Celtic temperament', as Heaney puts it.² Other stories come into my remembrance: childhood versions of the Children of Lir and the Return of Oisin, and innumerable other tales tied to particular places. They are tales of exquisite pain and nostalgia, even when the representatives of Christianity are more attractive than the intransigent, unsympathetic Bishop Ronan.

These stories involve people of the older race who return, after time-slip enchantments, to their previous world only to find it utterly altered by, amongst other things, the advent of Christianity. Lir's children, having completed their nine hundred years as storm-tossed wild swans, crumple and dwindle in a swift senescence as soon as they regain their human bodies. They lie helpless at the feet of Saint Kemoc, who baptises them promptly and tenderly before death overtakes them: a bittersweet ending.

But in *his* retelling of Oisin's story, 'The Wanderings of Oisin', Yeats will not have his Fenian hero submit so meekly to the new dispensation. His Oisin returns from three hundred years in the Isles of the Blest to find an elderly, tired Patrick, and a diminished people. He turns away from Patrick's 'bell-mounted churches', and grieves for what is lost:

> guardless the sacred
> cairn and the rath,
> And a small and feeble populace stooping with
> mattock and spade.³

Again and again such tales are placed in the pivotal period of Ireland's conversion. Saint Patrick the arch-missionary has left his firm foot in a thousand places throughout Ireland's five provinces, laying Christian claim to both individuals and sacred sites. He and his fellow-clerics took such decisive steps for Christ that all over Ireland they have left tangible imprints on stone that are reverenced still. These foot-shaped depressions hold pools of rainwater, and are commonly credited with healing powers.

The children of Lir go quietly, their years heavy upon them. Oisin turns away to a past that is already dismantled. Not so Sweeney. His transformation is the result not of Celtic magic, malign or otherwise, but of the new dispensation. After the psalter-throwing episode, Ronan calls down a curse on him, invoking it with the very bell that had so offended the king:

> it will curse you to the trees,
> bird-brain among branches.
>
> Section 10

And so it is that, in the form of a bird but with a man's consciousness, Sweeney wanders the length and breadth of Ireland and southern Scotland for many years.

They are long and most uncomfortable years, but Sweeney is not entirely comfortless during them. Unlike his persecutor he learns and changes radically. Henceforward he is both supplanted earthly king and 'king of the ditch-backs'; he is the captive of his madness and yet a freer spirit than any of the men and women who mock or despise him. The privations of his life in the wilderness open his warrior's senses to delight as well as to misery of body and mind. He learns to relish the way of life of the outcast, despite its human loneliness and physical distress. And he identifies, to a greater extent than any of the lyrical hermits of the early Irish nature poetry, with the life lived by the wild creatures who have become his companions.

By section 36 (of the text's 87), his foster or half-brother Lynchseachan can reproach him with having learnt to love his exile:

> Calm yourself. Come to. Rest.
> Come home east. Forget the west.
> Admit, Sweeney, you have come far
> from where your heart's affections are.
>
> Woods and forests and wild deer,

> now these things delight you more
> than sleeping in your eastern dun
> on a bed of feather down.
>
> Near a quick mill-pond, your perch
> on a dark green holly branch
> means more to you than any feast
> among the brightest and the best.

Sweeney's love for his country's wild places and creatures shines through the anguish of his imposed penance. The songs and soliloquies grow into a sort of informal *dinnseanchas*, the formal place-name poetry of the Celtic bards. And many of the places that are named and praised are for me, as for Heaney, already loved and familiar. Like him I grew up 'in sight of some of Sweeney's places and in earshot of others':[4] Slemish, the Mourne Mountains, Inishowen, Islandmagee. The known names sound through the text like the namings in a litany.

In its praise of them I begin to understand something more of the complexity of Heaney's involvement with this tale. For Sweeney is both a part of Heaney and also utterly other. The wildness of the Celtic king comes not only out of his recalcitrance, but out of something more chthonic. I am reminded of Heaney's paean to his own first place, the essay 'Mossbawn' in *Preoccupations*; and in particular a paragraph that tells of the moss – the bog – itself. It was

> forbidden ground. Two families lived at the heart of it,
> and a recluse, called Tom Tipping, whom we never
> saw, but in the morning on the road to school we
> watched his smoke rising from a clump of trees, and
> spoke his name between us until it was synonymous
> with mystery man, with unexpected scuttlings in the
> hedge, with footsteps slushing through long grass.

A strange congruence strikes me. I turn back to Poem I of 'Station Island' and re-read the stanzas that tell of the pilgrim's rejection of Simon Sweeney, the man who calls himself 'your mystery man':

> 'Stay clear of all processions!'
>
> Sweeney shouted at me
> but the murmur of the crowd
> and their feet slushing through
> the tender, bladed growth
> opened a drugged path
>
> I was set upon.

'The green spirit of the hedges embodied in Sweeney' is being excluded for the moment from the pilgrim's narrowing vision. Yet in the very sound and movement of the crowd he joins there is an echo of Tom Tipping, the unseen tutelary spirit of the bog that bounded his first world, that soft and fertile moss to which he felt himself 'betrothed' as a boy.[5] Here, though, childhood terrors are being left behind: now the slushing footsteps are those of the 'shawled women/ ... wading the young corn', the unindividualised female devotional crowd.

The pilgrim of 'Station Island' is summoned by the quick bell away from the solitary, nonconforming life of Sweeney, whether mad king or tinker. But what he is summoned to is not the simple warmth of community. 'Their motion saddened morning.' The memory of Heaney's childhood that lies behind this passage is of 'dark-garmented elders in an atmosphere of mourning'.[6] The women's unnamed sorrow and the inevitability of following them on their path through the trampled corn give the pilgrim's falling into step with them something of the tension that runs through the latter part of *Sweeney Astray*.

I return to *Sweeney Astray*, wanting to look again at Sweeney's purgatorial privations. I want to think more carefully about their penitential nature, for it seems that the relationship between the Christian and the pagan is more complex than I had at first perceived it. My natural inclination is to be more sympathetic to the pagan and to the defeated. But the shawled women in 'Station Island' may represent something more than the mindless rigmarole of cradle Catholicism, despite the adjective 'drugged'. They are after all in movement, not stationary, and they are located in the heart of the world of growth, not that indoor world of Christianity that made Alan Watts feel so un-at-home.

There is a comparable contradiction in the life of Sweeney. He accepts with saint-like grace the Christian shaping of his story, whilst living fully in the wild and pagan world of his exile. In section 32 he flies down on to the lintel of his wife's hunting cabin, and voices this acceptance for the first time:

EORANN   My poor tormented lunatic!
When I see you like this it makes me sick,
your cheek gone pale, your skin all scars,
ripped and scored by thorns and briars.

SWEENEY   And yet I hold no grudge,
my gentle one.
Christ ordained my bondage
and exhaustion.

After this acknowledgement of Christ's involvement in his predicament, Sweeney's trials increase. They become what one might expect in the medieval *Vita* of a saint. Soon his foster-brother Lynchseachan reminds him of all he has lost, using prose reminiscent of the *ubi sunt* passages popular in Christian Latin verse of the Middle Ages.

Do you remember your train, the lovely gentle women, the many young men and their hounds, the retinue of craftsmen? Do you remember the assemblies under your sway? Do you remember the cups and goblets and carved horns that flowed with pleasant

heady drink? It is a pity to find you like any poor bird
flitting from one waste ground to the next.

Section 35

It is a schooling in humility, a stripping away of the *hubris*
that Heaney himself recoils from: 'About the only *enmity* I
have is towards pride'.[7]

The stripping-down proceeds with a relentlessness that
is reminiscent of Jahweh's treatment of Job in the Old
Testament. Lynchseachan comes to the mad king with fresh
news: he tells Sweeney of the deaths of all his close family
in turn, culminating in that of his small son. This last grief
finally fells the bird-king from his perch, and puts him into
the power of Lynchseachan, who straitjackets him back to
sanity. Those stories, he is now told, are untrue, but the
shock and the confinement bring Sweeney to his senses
over a period of six weeks:

> ... his sense and memory came back to him ... So they
> took the tackle off him and he was back to his former
> self, the man they had known as king.

Section 37

The story, however, doesn't end there. After this short spell
of uneventful and confined sanity, Sweeney is precipitated
into madness again – and it tastes most gloriously of
freedom! The first utterance of this fresh onset of
'distraction' is the poem that has often been lifted from the
text as an anthology piece: his eloquent and joyous praise
of the trees of Ireland. And so a tension is set up between
the 'normal' world and that of the outsider which is almost
Laingian in its understanding of the mad person's
clearsightedness.

In this context, too, the penitential quality of Sweeney's
bird-life becomes a great contributor to his dignity. At times
it even takes on the feel of the famous penitential
pilgrimage itself:

I tread the slop
and foam of beds,
unlooked for,
penitential,

and imagine treelines
somewhere beyond,
a banked-up, soothing,
wooded haze,

not like the swung
depths and swells
of that nightmare-black
lough in Mourne.

Section 45

Treading the stone beds, a dark and forbidding lake – these
are images that bring Lough Derg to mind, and the thought
that for century after century Irish men and women, and
for a time pilgrims from all over Europe, have *chosen* to
experience a spell in this particular other- or underworld;
and been thought well of for having done it!

Ronan is implacable to the end, but Sweeney meets at
last a more 'Christian' saint, Moling. The closing days of his
life are recounted comparatively briefly, but in them several
interesting things occur. Firstly, Moling binds Sweeney to
return to him every evening, and writes down a record of
his adventures for posterity. Then, Sweeney has a singular
change from his obsessive diet of watercress:

Moling ordered his cook to leave aside some of each
day's milking for Sweeney's supper ... Sweeney's
supper was like this: she would sink her heel to the
ankle in the nearest cow-dung and fill the hole to the
brim with new milk. Then Sweeney would sneak into
the deserted corner of the milking yard and lap
it up.

Section 77

Lastly, Sweeney himself becomes tutelary spirit cum patron saint of all the places, especially the cress-topped springs, that he has visited and loved in his straying. Moling, who has 'limed him for the Holy Ghost', and drawn him close to the human world without trickery or violent 'cures', acknowledges Sweeney's spiritual growth and does not confine it within narrow definitions of creed:

> I ask a blessing, by Sweeney's grave.
> His memory flutters in my breast.
> His soul roosts in the tree of love.
> His body sinks in its clay nest.
>
> Section 85

Sweeney's last days bring together all his ambivalences. He is 'mad' to the last, but Moling the Christian cleric loves the places and actions of his madness:

> Wherever he
> migrated in flight from home
> will always be dear to me.
>
> Section 85

Sweeney, finally, is able to live in two worlds at once, the pagan and the Christian, the wild wood and the farmed world. The dairy farm, where he sups milk from dung, is a place with its own ambivalence because of the earlier existence of dairying's patron saint, Brigid, as a Celtic fertility goddess. He breathes his last at the very door of Moling's church, never entering under its roof, and yet he has collaborated in the cloister-work of writing down his story.

What runs consistently through all these ambivalences is Sweeney's aloneness, his pre-existential consciousness of his individuality. Is it then Sweeney the outsider, the one who must find his own salvation in solitude and away from mankind, that Heaney leaves behind so summarily in the first poem of 'Station Island'? There will be penance enough for the pilgrim on the island purgatory, but there will be no solitude. The only wildness will be in the ring of almost habitationless hills on the lough's horizon.

Joining the procession means giving up the 'migrant solitude' of 'The King of the Ditchbacks', the poem that completes Part One of the collection *Station Island*. It means returning to the world of dependence, of childhood, of community. It means going down among the women, into a field full of female folk with, in the lines of Poem I, 'half-remembered faces, / a loosed congregation / that straggled past and on'. It is above all a renunciation of singularity and of pride.

*   *   *

Are, then, the female and the humble inextricably linked for Heaney? It is a link learned in the religious devotions of his childhood, especially through their 'generally Marian quality'. In the same interview in which he voiced his 'enmity' towards pride, he set it in this context:

> A religion that has a feminine component and a notion of the mother in the transcendent world is better than a religion that just has a father, a man, in it. I also - just in my nature and temperament, I suppose - believed in humility and in bowing down, and in 'we' rather than 'I'. I hate a moi situation, egotism, a presumption, a hubris, and I'm used to bowing down to the mother as a way of saying that.[8]

I understand what he is saying, and yet for me, as a woman, it is precisely that 'offer it up' mentality that has made me turn away from the same religion, and in particular from the female model it offers. The phrase 'bowing down to the mother' raises for me all the problems I have with the ideal and myth of Mary, the immaculately

conceived and asexually conceiving virgin-mother. I see
these problems not just in relation to myself as a woman,
but in the way men, and Irish men in particular, relate to
the women in their lives. As Marina Warner says in the
Epilogue to her extensive and elegant study of the myth of
Mary:

> She is the symbol of the ideal woman and has been
> held up as an example to women since Tertullian in
> the third century and John Chrysostom in the fourth
> lambasted the sex. The imitation of the perfected
> female type of humanity is still enthusiastically
> encouraged in Catholic families and schools from
> Ireland to Brazil ... Mary establishes the child as the
> destiny of woman, but escapes the sexual intercourse
> necessary for all other women to fulfil this destiny.
> Thus the very purpose of women established by the
> myth with one hand is slighted with the other. The
> Catholic religion therefore binds its female followers in
> particular on a double wheel, to be pulled one way
> and then the other ... on the one hand [Catholicism]
> affirms the beauty and goodness of the the the natural
> world ... on the other it endorses the most pessimistic
> world-denying self-sacrifice as the state of the elect.[9]

In Ireland the whole issue is further complicated, of course,
by the perceived feminine presence of Ireland itself,
whether seen as 'Mother Ireland' or 'Kathleen ni Houlihan',
idealised maternal figure or idealised maiden.

I am saddened anew by Heaney-the-pilgrim's turning
away from the figure of Sweeney, even if it is expressed
here only in the limited persona of the tinker Simon
Sweeney, non-joiner and sabbath-breaker. For I delight, as
I feel Heaney himself does, in the recalcitrance of Sweeney.
I rejoice in his love of place, his allegiance to the west. I
have fought all my adult life to free myself of the reflexes
of humility, have had to learn to be 'self-centred'. I ponder
the implications for Heaney-as-artist in this joining of an

undifferentiated murmuring crowd. And worry about what sort of female presence that crowd represents.

In the introduction to *Sweeney Astray* Heaney writes: '... insofar as Sweeney is also a figure of the artist, displaced, guilty, assuaging himself by his utterance, it is possible to read the work as an aspect of the quarrel between free creative imagination and the constraints of religious, political and domestic obligation.' I know that Heaney's first shot at translating the medieval text was when he had just moved from Belfast to rural seclusion in County Wicklow in the autumn of 1972:

> I am neither internee nor informer;
> An inner émigré, grown long-haired
> And thoughtful; a wood-kerne
>
> Escaped from the massacre,
> Taking protective colouring
> From bole and bark, feeling
> Every wind that blows; ...[10]

In that flitting, and in the singling out of *Buile Suibhne* as a focus for his attention, he had seemed to me to be aligning himself unquestionably with the 'free creative imagination'; and donning, metaphorically at least, the bird cloak traditionally associated with ancient Irish bards. It was a romantic image. Now, in choosing the path to Station Island, he and I, however reluctantly, must take into our reckoning just those 'constraints of religious, political and domestic obligation' that we would both gladly shrug off in a flight into the wilderness.

*   *   *

I close the dark green covers of *Sweeney Astray*. Two admonitions – both in Heaney's hand, though in each case

put in another character's mouth – will not leave me in
peace: Simon Sweeney's 'Stay clear of all processions' and
Lynchseachan's 'Come home east. Forget the west.'

Tomorrow is our last day in Donegal. We must pack up
in the morning and drive east across Ulster to Belfast. For
Michael it will be a first visit to that city. For me it will be
a return home after twenty-two years of half-intentional
exile. Although I have been returning for several years to
Ireland's west, to the Atlantic coast from Donegal in the
north down to Clare and the cliffs of Moher, and inland too
to my mother's family farm in East Galway, I have often
skirted round the Six Counties, avoiding border-crossings,
and have revisited the house and city of my childhood only
in dreams.

Frost still holds in the morning. Soil and vegetation have
contracted a little further. Iniskeel lies opposite, the colour
of drought in the gilding of the low sun. But the moon has
still not increased enough towards the full: we must leave
the island unstepped on, as we left Station Island the
previous day, scanned from a distance across dividing
waters.

We drive north-east from Gweebarra into the Aghla
mountains, and as we go along the northern shore of high
Lough Finn, whose waters are held in the pass, I remember
my father taking me to a wet place somewhere in these
hills when I was a child, and telling me that here was the
watershed, the place where the water decided whether it
would run west to the Gweebarra River and the Atlantic,
or east to the Finn and so finally into the River Foyle and
then north into Lough Foyle. Today we are set on that
latter journey, to the city of Derry that is built on both
banks of the Foyle, though the half of its natural hinterland
that is County Donegal was lost to it in the Partition of
1922.

We cross the river into the Six Counties at Lifford /
Strabane, past a heavily sandbagged military post and a
no-man's-land of broken concrete and failed petrol stations,
and head for Derry to call on my aunt by marriage. She

moved back here, to her native city, after her husband's death in Belfast. He was a Catholic judge there, the one murdered in the hall of his home by 'a shut-eyed boy' that Tom Paulin wrote of in his seventies poem 'Under the Eyes'.[11] We werè all near neighbours when I lived in Belfast, she and I Catholics, Paulin a Protestant, living on three parallel streets in the city's south side. Not one of us lives there now.

We talk of the continuing loss and fracturing that have followed on my uncle's death, for the province as well as his family. And we talk of the past and future of the Republicanism in which my aunt was brought up in Derry, and about which she is now so disillusioned. Too much has been martyred to it, she says, on every level. She stands outside all politics now, but she cannot conceive of living outside her country. She is of Ulster, like it or not. Of her children, one is working in the South, the other in London.

I mention Heaney's name. Many of her male contemporaries went to Heaney's old school, Saint Columb's College in Derry, and yes, she's been to a reading of his recently in the City. She's no poetry buff, she says, but she can recognise her land through the clear windows of his poems. Her talk soon moves on to the complacency of those so-called republicans of Derry City who are happy to combine no-go areas for the British with a complacent and cynical acceptance of their social security pay-outs. And where will be an end to it?

We say our goodbyes and drive on soberly east, out over the new Foyle bridge that she can see from her picture window. As a gesture against other sobrieties, I suggest to Michael a detour to Bushmills, home of the famous Irish malt .whiskey. I have not remembered that it will be Protestant heartland. But as we enter the village, the clear message of the red, white and blue kerbstones that define its central crossroads and of the anti-papist slogans on the walls of its buildings wakens childhood terror in me. This territorial cheek of the Protestant paint-brush suddenly makes sense of my being troubled by that other admonition of Simon Sweeney: 'Stay clear of all processions.'

Of course – processions secular, as well as processions religious! Until this moment I have been thinking of Marian devotions, of childhood Corpus Christi processions in the sunlit gardens of my first school, a Dominican convent in Belfast. I have been remembering the chosen ones walking backwards in blue-sashed dresses and strewing rhododendron and rose petals before the Christ-filled monstrance; the lovely wind-caught diminuendi of hymns sung in the open air; the makeshift altar under the sky. But there are other processions in my childhood too, ones that I meant to keep clear of, but didn't.

In Belfast we lived one long street away from the Lisburn Road. When I was at the big-girls' school, I walked through to catch my bus there. But long before that I would sneak down there on one particular day in the summer of every year, and climb carefully inside a thick hedge that faced on to the main road. The day was the Twelfth of July, and the Lisburn Road was part of the main route of the Orange marches.

My terror and my fascination were indistinguishable to me as a small child, cowering in that hedge. The heavy, almost subsonic beat of the huge Lambeg drums, the restless sopranino of the fifes, and the tread of a thousand stern bowler-hatted men were like whole-body pins and needles, or wasps in my blood. I sank lower in the hedge, wondering what would happen if the X-ray vision of an Orange baton twirler were to penetrate my hide, and know instantly – of course – that I was a Catholic.

And yet I could not stay away! To this day any marching music with that same combination of heavy drumbeats and high whistles makes me jumpy as a bonfire-night cat, whatever the 'side' of the marchers. I am chilled by it but also stirred in a way I do not understand or like. There seems to be some strange correspondence between my fascinated recoil from the physical presence of Station Island, with its associations of mass devotion, and from the atavistic beat of the Orange marches. Is it a fascination, unacknowledged in my conscious mind, with the pull of community, a gut-response to the visible sense of safe and favoured belonging that living within those 'constraints of religious, political and domestic obligation' can offer?

In the North of Ireland, that pull of community is polarised to an extent that is hard to remember when one has lived away for years. But it is utterly part of my own divided childhood, and so of me. I *want* to say: 'A plague on both your houses! I'd rather stay out in the wilderness and the wet!' By returning at long last to the Six Counties, and reaching them troubled by the questions raised in Heaney's long poem, I know I can no longer put off an exploration of the first world that, like it or not, is my inheritance.

We reverse the car from Bushmills' tiny centre. We do not even wish to visit the distillery now, but see its pagoda-like malt kilns in the distance as we accelerate out of town. Then it's south-east by south as fast as we can – there is snow in the air, and not many hours left of light.

NOTES

1. *Sweeney Astray*, sections 3 & 4.
2. In his Introduction.
3. *Collected Poems*, 2nd edn, p. 443.
4. Introduction, *Sweeney Astray*.
5. See *Preoccupations*, p.19.
6. In a letter about this passage, Seamus Heaney wrote: 'The memory behind that goes back to early childhood: a field through which a short cut ran to a small footbridge that led people across the Moyola river to the church at Newbridge. That field, being traversed in a straggled sort of way by dark-garmented elders in an atmosphere of mourning, always remained somewhere in my memory.'
7. John Haffenden, *Viewpoints: Poets in Conversation*, p.61.
8. Ibid., p.61.
9. *Alone of All Her Sex*, pp.336-7.
10. 'Exposure' in *North*.

11.   'But he wasn't "shut-eyed" at all,' says my aunt. 'Tom Paulin got that wrong. He had the most beautiful eyes, brilliant blue eyes. And they were open wide as he fired.'

CHAPTER FOUR

Hammering Home the Shape of Things

Poem II

11 January 1987: Driving east
2 August 1987: On the bus to Lough Derg

'... And always, Orange drums.
And neighbours on the roads at night with guns.'

'Station Island', Poem II

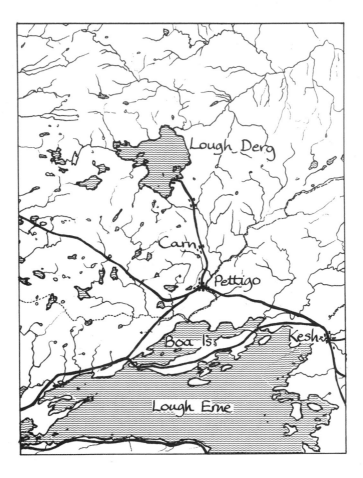

Lough Erne & Lough Derg

January the eleventh. The high light of a cloudless dusk is rubbed raw and red by columns of snow – they are lit by sunset, and draw its red light high into the failing blue of sub-zero air. They are showers like the pillars of rain I have sometimes seen blowing towards me as I sit on a sea cliff in the west: self-sufficient flurries of precipitation that seem to require no cloud structure above them.

I am driving fast along Ulster's M2, a road unknown to me that now cuts heartlessly through the intimate scale of the Antrim countryside. It will take us, almost before I realise it, deep into the dockland area of Belfast. And these hills that are marched on by the columns of red-stained snow are the western shoulders of Divis, and Black Mountain, and now the black snout of Cave Hill. I recognise the swinging skyline of their unchanging shapes above the unrecognisable road system. The wind gusts across the motorway, and snow is suddenly flying at us in the headlamps' beams. I am returning home in *Sweeney Astray* weather, 'piercingly exposed to the beauties and severities of the natural world',[1] but with my mind full of images of people slushing through young corn, or marching in the season of the deep-throated orange lily . . .

*   *   *

Heaney the pilgrim, too, is seated at the wheel of his car, though it is not moving except in the buffeting of the wind. It is parked on one of those long and lonely roads that rides across the hill country of southern Ulster. But the poet who has so often found that the 'real' roads seen through a windscreen have 'unreeled, unreeled'[2] his meditations on the *cammin di nostra vita*[3] finds himself on his feet again, though not processing.

For in the second poem of the 'Station Island' sequence, Heaney, along with the rhythmic and blurry first world of community, is tipped out rudely on to the tarmac of politics.

               I was suddenly out
        face to face with an aggravated man

        raving on about nights spent listening for
        gun butts to come cracking on the door,
        yeomen on the rampage, and his neighbour

        among them, hammering home the shape of things.

William Carleton, essayist and novelist extraordinaire,
strides purposefully out of the nineteenth century to put
'this cub' right about the meaning of community. The
crowd of shawled women with their 'Pray for us, pray for
us' would have felt themselves part of the 'communion of
saints', the vast assembly of the souls of all the living and
dead in Catholic Christendom. But the living memory of
violence cuts across their chanting, breaks step with the
summons of the quick bell. These are real bodies that
Carleton speaks of: he says he

        smelled hanged bodies rotting on their gibbets
        and saw their looped slime gleaming from the sacks –

Real as the mutilated skull of my own second cousin,
'executed' in east Galway by the Black and Tans in 1921,
who was dragged home head down behind the police lorry,
and thrown into his mother's yard; real as my uncle,
gunned down in his own front hall in Belfast in 1975. Real
as every victim 'slashed and dumped' since the old
Troubles reawoke in the North in the late sixties. Every
family, Protestant or Catholic, north or south of the Border,
has its own roll-call, its martyrology.

    What Carleton also introduces to the poem is anger, and
the argument of action's necessity, whether literal or
metaphorical:

        If times were hard, I could be hard too.
        I made the traitor in me sink the knife.

Against this is set the at first unvoiced rejoinder of the passive – the smile, with something defensive about it, that Carleton notes on Heaney the pilgrim's face.

Heaney calls William Carleton 'a Tyrone Virgil' in *Preoccupations*, and here he is, muscling his way in at the start of Heaney's dream pilgrimage. Heaney is not Dante, nor Carleton his pagan guide; and when the older man turns on his heel at the end of the poem, it is not even clear whether he is continuing in the same direction as Heaney. But both the setting and the dialogue of this meeting, miles still from Lough Derg, raise questions and sensitivities in the pilgrim that he will explore, painfully, on the island – in Carleton's determined absence.

*   *   *

Carleton's is a strange story. One summer *circa* 1812, a young lad 'of quick perception – warm imagination – a mind peculiarly romantic – a morbid turn for devotion, and a candidate for the priesthood' (his own description) set out on foot from his parents' farm in the parish of Clogher in County Tyrone to 'do his station' at Lough Derg. By the most direct route – and the traces of centuries-old pilgrim ways still survive in the wild country that surrounds Lough Derg – this was a walk of not less than thirty-five miles, west by north. He started out at six in the morning and walked his bare feet 'to griskins' on the stone and gravel – good preparation for Purgatory.

Whenever I re-read William Carleton's autobiographical essay 'The Lough Derg Pilgrim', I am struck by its ironies. For it records not just the contemporary conduct of the historic pilgrimage with a fine mixture of anger, compassion and humour, but the consequent loss of that morbid and romantic lad's priestly vocation. And it was the publication of this vivid and contentious essay that was to make Carleton's name as a writer, 'overnight' as they say,

in 1828. In the intervening years he had converted from his
native Catholicism to the church of the Protestant and
Anglo-Irish Ascendancy – which may have helped. (As a
child in Ireland I was told by the nuns of conversions only
the other way: they *always* helped!)

When Heaney sets out on the ancient pilgrim way from
'home' to Lough Derg, he finds that he shares at least the
first part of the road with William Carleton. Although some
of their choices as adults were significantly different, the
two men were similar in their rural Ulster Catholic
upbringing and early academic promise; like Carleton,
Heaney has become a writer for and of his people, a writer
who conveys their spirit with a particular and often critical
authenticity. He, too, has become a 'best-seller' across Saint
George's Channel as well as in his native land. But
suddenly he hears his mentor say: 'It is a road you travel
on your own ...' Heaney cannot, any more than Carleton,
continue in the simplicities of his childhood. Looked back
on from this wind-buffeted mountain road, that field of
womenfolk seems to offer only the unquestioned tuggings
and comforts of early infancy.

Carleton is right. In the North of Ireland there are two
very distinct understandings of 'community', that of the
'hard-mouthed Ribbonmen' and that of the 'Orange bigots'.
There is no place that is free of this divisiveness, as Heaney
is bound to agree. And like it or not, all those that grow up
in the province take it in, as one might say, with their
mother's milk.

The part played by women in this first world and its
rites of transition is unmistakably in Heaney's mind in this
encounter. Carleton's essay is chiefly read for its detailed
account of the pilgrimage devotions and the Purgatory's
'prison' that imitates death, and for its eloquent attack on
the heartless simony of a priest on the island. Heaney the
pilgrim calls to mind none of that expected material in this
meeting with Carleton's ghost, but rather the framing story
of the 1812 walk to and from Lough Derg – and the two
tricksy old women who became, willy-nilly, Carleton's

companions on the road.

The two men hold their out-of-time dream meeting on a mountain only a few miles from Carleton's home in County Tyrone. The first words quoted from their dream conversation identify it as the place where Carleton overtook the very women who became his fawning and over-zealous companions, and who ultimately played a large part in his disillusionment. They seemed to be devout pilgrims, speaking counterparts of the shawled processors of Poem I of Heaney's sequence, but they were in reality light-fingered 'shulers', women of the road. They knew they had chanced on an easy prey, and made sure they travelled back on the same road with him. In 'The Lough Derg Pilgrim', Carleton describes how, when he returned home minus all his money and his outer clothes, after a last night spent at the same lodging-house as the two women, he learned that one of them was 'Nell McCollum, the most notorious shuler in the province! a gipsy, a fortune-teller, and a tinker's widow.'

Woman as trickster and traitor, woman as warm home-presence: it's an old dichotomy. In Carleton's story it is a travelling woman – a female counterpart of the tinker Simon Sweency? – who lightens him of his possessions. She also lightens the young man he was of his vocation to the priesthood, and plays a part in the loss of his cradle Catholicism. It was, of course, Carleton's extreme hostility to that faith and all its works that endeared him to his (Protestant) readership from 1828 onwards (the year in which his essay 'The Lough Derg Pilgrim' was published in *The Christian Examiner*). And yet it was his intimate knowledge and understanding of the peasant (and so Catholic) population from which he sprang that ensured his continuing popularity. The very basis of his creativity as a writer is this split within his history, and within his self. The anger which is his most emphatic characteristic in Heaney's portrayal of him is a microcosm of the conflict between Catholic and Protestant, between native and settler, between the female and male sides of his soul.

One half of one's sensibility is in a cast of mind that comes from belonging to a place, an ancestry, a history, a culture, whatever one wants to call it. But consciousness and quarrels with the self are the results of what Lawrence called 'the voices of my education'.[4]

Carleton's quarrel with himself darkened over the years, and the two conflicting admonitions he gives to the pilgrim whose early history and fosterage is so like his own are: anger *and* acceptance.

> If times were hard, I could be hard too.
> I made the traitor in me sink the knife.
> And maybe there's a lesson there for you,

he cries at first, but later offers a reconciliation that he may or may not have achieved in his own work:

> Remember everything and keep your head.

Carleton prefaces the revised edition of *Traits and Stories of the Irish Peasantry* (the collection of essays in which 'The Lough Derg Pilgrim' was published in book form) with an account of his 'own youth, early station in society, and general education, as the son of an honest humble peasant.' Not only is the account a wholly affectionate one, but it shows that the basis of Carleton's gifts and material as a storyteller was unquestionably laid down at that humble hearth in Tyrone.

> [My father's] memory was a perfect storehouse, and a rich one, of all that the social antiquary, the man of letters, the poet, or the musician, would consider valuable ... I have hardly ever since, heard, [sic] during a tolerably enlarged intercourse with Irish 'society, both educated and uneducated – with the antiquary, the scholar, or the humble senachie – any single tradition, usage, or legend, that ... was perfectly

new to me.

His mother gave him the ancient music of Ireland, and more:

This gift of singing with such sweetness and power the old sacred songs and airs of Ireland, was not the only one for which she was remarkable. Perhaps there never lived a human being capable of giving the Irish cry, or Keene, with such exquisite effect, or of pouring into its wild notes a spirit of such irresistible pathos and sorrow.

Despite this noble tribute, and Carleton's stated intention of presenting the Irishman as something other than the ridiculous and ill-spoken buffoon of popular report, his essays themselves betray a constant mismatch of intention and achievement. At times his transliterations of Irish peasant pronunciation and his accounts of their gullibility ally him more closely to the colonial and patronising attitudes of his near contemporary and adopted co-religionist, Thomas Crofton Croker, a descendent of Elizabethan settlers in Cork who was the first collector and publisher of the texts of Irish folktales: he called his pursuit a 'sport', and wrote that he was 'hunting up and bagging all the old "grey superstitions".'[5]

When Carleton strides fast 'in his sure haste along the crown of the road' towards Heaney's parked car, and engages him in rueful conversation, he describes himself as 'the old fork-tongued turncoat'. As they talk, the younger man gradually becomes the gentle mentor of the older, who has long since been living far away from 'the dark mountains and green vales of [his] native Tyrone'. For, like Heaney, he too had moved to the big city, to Dublin.

What Heaney offers to him with increasing confidence is a renewed commitment to that rural first world whose image is darkened and deepened now by their shared awareness of its innate divisions. It is as Carleton calms

down during the recital of the youthful experiences they
share, despite the hundred and forty-odd year difference in
their births (in itself a testimony to the enduring folk
tradition in Ireland), that he is able to offer the redeeming
advice to 'Remember everything'. Heaney the pilgrim
responds to this in his turn, re-entering like a triggered
somnambulist the sensuous world of *Death of a Naturalist*,
its soft mulch and fingered slime:

> 'The alders in the hedge,' I said, 'mushrooms,
> dark-clumped grass where cows or horses dunged,
> the cluck when pith-lined chestnut shells split open
>
> in your hand, the melt of shells corrupting,
> old jampots in a drain clogged up with mud –'

'Remember' – the advice put into Carleton's mouth is an
almost-invocation of the Muses, who are, after all, the
daughters of Memory: this is, perhaps, Heaney's shy and
hidden version of the sort of invocation that traditionally
prefaces an epic poem. His sequence's modesty rules out
such *hubris* at its opening, but the very movement of the
poem, its *Prelude*-like concern for seedtime, itself enacts a
sort of summoning of the muse.

Carleton's final words before he turns on his heel
suggest that he too experiences once again the cleansing
power of the natural world, and the equilibrium that its
cycle of fertility and decay can demonstrate even to the
turncoat, the city-dweller, the man who has moved
inexorably into the world of Blake's 'Experience'. Both men
have hard and solitary journeys to make, on metalled road
and bare stone, but in their parting they are closer to the
field of green growing of Poem I, and to sympathy with
each other, than seemed possible at the poem's brusque and
tarmac beginning.

For Heaney's words also counter Carleton's earlier
urging of the necessity to *act* angrily, out of a just anger.
His mud and dung-rich quietism raises questions that will

be returned to throughout the rest of the sequence. How far
is it right and just to be passive in a time and a place like
Ireland in the eighties? To what extent is that passivity a
part of the long history of being a subject race, and to what
extent can it be seen as that 'wise passiveness, a surrender
to energies that spring within the centre of the mind' that
Heaney so admires in his reading of the opening passage
of Wordsworth's *Prelude*?[6] And for Heaney there is the
other post-Partition pressure of silence, the gag all Catholic
citizens of the Six Counties must deal with one way or the
other:

> Northern reticence, the tight gag of place
> And times: yes, yes. Of the 'wee six' I sing
> Where to be saved you must only save face
> And whatever you say, you say nothing.[7]

The pilgrimage to Lough Derg traditionally starts the
moment you leave your own door, and ends on your
return. The journey, and the fasting that must be observed
on it, are as much a part of the pilgrimage as the time spent
on the island itself. I see all of a sudden that it can have a
solitary element as well as all that communality:

> It is a road you travel on your own.

Heaney's poem is structured by that pilgrimage; it also
follows the movements of autobiography. But the 'seedtime
of [his] soul' is not uniformly 'fair': the young growth is
both 'tender' and 'bladed'. Attending to his own voice
carries with it the possibility, in Catholic terms, of the very
hubris he has been schooled to hate. When Christian, at the
beginning of *Pilgrim's Progress*, ran from his door and from
his family, he 'put his fingers in his ears, and ran on,
crying, Life! life! eternal life! So he looked not behind him,
but fled towards the middle of the plain.' Neither for
Heaney nor for Carleton is such a total conversion
experience possible. In their different ways the writings of

both men have been fed by the conflict between their nurture and their chosen exile. The difference is in the level of their consciousness of the workings of this conflict.

To trust one's own self and voice can be, in a Catholic world-picture, dangerously close to the sin of Lucifer. The pilgrim Heaney goes on into the Underworld, into his vision of Purgatory, without any guide but his own self-doubt. There will be no Sibyl as for Aeneas, no Virgil or Beatrice as for Dante, no one to lead him or to elucidate his visions. He utters no invocation to Christ, or even to that chief intercessor, Mary. It is the sights and feels and smells of his mud-pie-making childhood that he holds on to as talismans to take into the dark.

NOTES

1. 'Introduction', *Sweeney Astray*.
2. 'Westering', the last poem in *Wintering Out*.
3. From the opening line of Dante's Inferno ('the path of our life').
4. *Preoccupations*, p.35.
5. Henry Glassie, *Irish Folktales*, p.11.
6. *Preoccupations*, p. 63.
7. 'Whatever You Say Say Nothing III', in *North*.

PART TWO

On Station Island

CHAPTER FIVE

Habit's Afterlife

Poem III

2 August 1987: 3 p.m.
Crossing to the Island

> *Qual negligenza, quale stare e questo?*
> *Correte al monte a spogliarvi lo scoglio,*
> *ch'esser non lascia a voi Dio manifesto.*

> Why this negligence? why this hanging back?
> Run to the mountain, strip yourselves of filth
> That will not let you see God clearly.

Purgatorio, II. 121-3

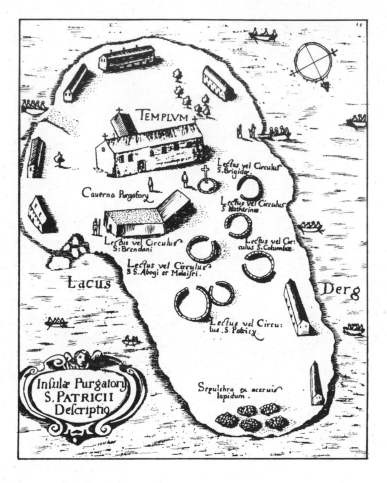

Station Island, after Carve's map in *Lyra Hibernica, 1666*

The leaf and flower of high summer have transformed even the desolate boglands and unforested hills near Lough Derg. Past Pettigo the fields of snug grazing peter out into moor, but the ditches are bright with the tall clusters of August's white and cream: meadowsweet, wild angelica, moon-carrot. The large leaves of the hazels give weight to bony hedges. When the sun springs out and races after the cloud-shadows, a hundred different greens spring out with it in the moorland's bands and shadings of bracken, sphagnum, fescues and rushes.

I have come on the pilgrims' bus to Lough Derg to 'do my station' as a sort of duty – I am not sure at this moment to what or to whom. And this second journey here, this *turas*, is necessarily done on my own. Like my solitary secular journeys to Donegal's south-west coast, it is one of those rare but essential times when I am no one but myself: not mother, not lover, not wife; not even friend, not even writer. Do I miss my daughters, or Michael? No. Once I am across the channel of dividing sea, those links seem to fall away and my consciousness is untrammelled even by love. But this trip has the unaccustomed addition of company. Already I am breathing in the sweetness in the air that comes from the courtesies of my fellow-Catholics. It is another sort of love, an acceptance. And I accept willingly in return, although with it I am signing away a large part of my preferred solitude.

Is it the softening of summer, or is this landscape altered by the inner eye? I call to mind the stark description of the scene by William Carleton's Protestant mentor, Caesar Otway:

> Lough Derg under my feet – the lake, the shores, the mountains, the accompaniments of all sorts presented the very landscape of desolation ... A person who had never seen the picture that was now under my eye, who had read of a place consecrated by the devotion of ages, towards which the tide of human superstition had flowed for twelve centuries, might imagine that St

Patrick's Purgatory, secluded in its sacred island,
would have all the venerable and gothic
accompaniments of olden time: and its ivied towers
and belfried steeples, its carved windows, and
cloistered arches, its long dark aisles and fretted vaults
would have risen out of the water, rivalling Iona or
Lindisfarn [sic]; but nothing of the sort was to be seen
... the whole prospect before me struck my mind with
a sense of painfulness, and I said to myself, 'I am
already in Purgatory'.[1]

And that was the closest to the Purgatory that he came.
He never set foot on the island, as I shall do in a very few
minutes. He was not a believer, nor ever had been, unlike
his protégé.

No, the Reverend Caesar Otway is not the man to see it
as I do on this day of pilgrimage. In January I might have
been more in sympathy with him, but now I have slipped
easily into step with my companions. I am aware, too, of
the years of persecution that removed any chance of gothic
charm surviving on the island, often literally: for instance,
in 1632 one thousand pounds sterling was expended on the
utter destruction of the Lough Derg stones, including the
ones in the water that St Patrick was held to have marked
with his knees and feet. The stones were thrown into the
lake or taken away altogether; the island was declared
forbidden ground. This destruction was personally
supervised by the Anglican Bishop of Clogher. The modern
buildings may not be ivied and fretted, but the faith that
has rebuilt and rebuilt through all those centuries'
vicissitudes is alive on this day, and I am a part of it.

On the bus, there is a rising excitement. People strain to
get a first glimpse of the lough, like children vying to be
the first to cry 'I see the sea!' This is a holiday, both in the
original sense of holy day, and in the sense of a time away
from work, away from home. After the long journey we
loosen limbs, laugh, renew conversations that had faltered
into dozing in the crossing of the midlands. When at last

we swing downhill towards the lough and its islands, the new hostel rises like a pillar of bright Carrara marble on the western side. Was this the grey half-finished building that I found so oppressive and prison-like back in January? It is to replace the existing women's hostel, I am told by a proud fellow passenger – and isn't it great the way the money is pouring in from all corners of Ireland for the building fund?

Because it is Sunday, our bus left Bus Aras an hour later than the usual starting time, and the driver has been racing over the last miles of the narrow, bucking bog-road to get us to the ferry in time. The last boat leaves for the island at three o'clock. Purgatory has been open to this day's new pilgrims since eleven. 'The lucky devils,' grumbles my new-found friend inappropriately, 'they'll have their three stations done and be taking their ease, gawping at the likes of us!' For, late or not, she tells me, every pilgrim must complete three rounds of the penitential prayers round the stone beds and the basilica before nightfall on the first day.

The boat is waiting for us when we step eagerly down from the bus, but first we must sign in and pay for our stay on the island: ten pounds sterling or eleven Irish punts. In return I am given a great silvery token – a light aluminium 'coin' about an inch and a half across – to give to the ferryman. I had not expected anything so symbolic, and am reluctant to part with it so soon; but I must walk down straightaway to the landing-stage and hand it to a lad who is, I hope, unaware of the odd look I give him. Does he know about Charon, about coins for the ferryman . . . ?

It is impossible, however, to be the slightest bit morbid in the company that packs into the fifty-seater open boat. We have joined other pilgrims, and the crack is off again – where we are from, how many times we have been before – the fools that we are. And what will the good Lord do to us in the way of weather? The wind is cold off the water and there's a shower darkening the western shore, but the journey takes only a few minutes. We are already across the short channel before the squall reaches us. The lad I cast

momentarily as Charon hoists us and our small
hand-luggage over the boat's gunwale. We are on the
concrete, and will soon be on the soil, of Station Island.

It is like entering a part of a city – a part where there is
no traffic and no shops, only a quickly forgotten booth for
religious items and cards near the landing-stage. We walk
into a lawned and paved open space between tall buildings,
and hundreds of people of all ages and conditions are in it
and round it, some clearly preoccupied, others strolling or
at rest. No, not all ages: there are no babies or children, of
course, for no one under the age of fourteen can do the
pilgrimage. Their absence gives the gathering a sober air,
and for me an immediate one of estrangement from the
everyday.

There is remarkably little noise: no raised voices, no
music. Some people are talking and even laughing here and
there, but those who are in the midst of prayers move their
lips silently. Wide flights of steps at the far end of this
almost-piazza lead the eye to the open doors of the basilica;
the small area of lumpy broken ground and bare rock to
the right must contain – yes – the low circular walls that
are the famous stone 'beds' of the saints. Hardly visible
from here, except for the little inlet at the foot of the 'beds',
is the wild water of the lough and the inhospitable ring of
hills.

We hurry to our respective hostels, men to the left,
women on and to the right, for we must quickly claim our
cubicles and strip the coverings from our feet. We are
greeted at the door of the women's hostel, and given our
bed numbers. I'm in cubicle number 190, on the second
floor. It's such a maze of similar corridors and curtained
compartments that I write the number in biro on my hand
as a reminder. The tongue-and-grooved partitions painted
cream, the iron bedsteads with their hammocked mat-
tresses, the harsh linen and wool of the bedding – oh, these
are familiar. I take a perverse pleasure in the thought of
spending one more night – tomorrow night, not this night,
of course – in the gratefully forgotten world of my convent

boarding-school.

Shoes and socks come off and are pushed with my rucksack behind the iron bedhead. My needs are few: the clothes I stand up in, a windproof cagoule for the night watches, and the leaflet that details the penitential exercises.

Walking barefoot indoors first of all, on composition corridors and stone stairs, and on the unattractively damp floor of a lavatory, removes much of the feel of ancientness that I have been expecting. In my imagined station I have only walked, painfully but romantically, on the stone 'beds'. Outside, lawn-grass and paving-stones begin to console my disappointed feet with their more wholesome textures. I cross the open space, each step feelingly taken, to start my first station according to the sheet of exercises. There is no time to lose:

> Begin the Station with a visit to the Blessed
> Sacrament in Saint Patrick's Basilica.

The simple and spacious beauty of the almost unadorned interior takes me by surprise. Here is none of the Italianate accoutrements of piety that have marred the aesthetics of post-Famine Irish Catholicism. Another tradition is here, the plain lines of a conception worthy of the place's antiquity: Irish-Romanesque. I discover later that its architect, W.A. Scott, conceived the plan of the octagonal building 'in the space of a night and a day spent on the island' in 1919 – a fruitful vigil.[2]

There is little time, however, for that sort of contemplation. I am to learn very fast that the conduct of this pilgrimage does not encourage meditation: a great part of its penitential nature, as far as I am concerned, lies in the endless demands of its mind-numbing exercises. And I realise with dismay that I have forgotten to pack the essential equipment for performing a part of these – a rosary. If I were a proper, a practising Catholic, my rosary would be as inseparable from me as my wallet or my watch. Unable to unearth my old rosary of Connemara

marble from twenty years of house-moves and accretions,
I bought a new cheap one specially for now. I can see the
corner of my desk in England where it is sitting at this
moment. But I *have* seen another one, nearer to hand . . .

Moments later I am back up on the landing of the hostel,
waiting for the coast to clear. Silence above and below me.
I stretch up and unhook a broken rosary of blue glass from
the praying hands of a near life-size plaster statue of Our
Lady. It hooks back together easily, and I gently bite the
link closed, pleased to discover that it has lost not a decade,
not a single Hail Mary, from its complement. I can return
to my station the compleat pilgrim – externally at any rate.

*   *   *

> I knelt. Hiatus. Habit's afterlife . . .
> I was back among bead clicks and the murmurs
> from inside confessionals, side altars
> where candles died insinuating slight
>
> intimate smells of wax at body heat.

Heaney the pilgrim does not tell of the boat crossing, the
coin for the ferryman, the winds low over the waters. In
Poem III, the first of the sequence set on the Island, he
kneels at once in the airless heart of indoor worship,
amongst the smells and sounds and warmth of votive
candles, and the suggested presences of those who have lit
them. But the church of these opening lines is nothing like
the basilica on Station Island. This is a vision from the past,
both Heaney's own and Lough Derg's.

For these lines conjure up the atmosphere in Saint
Mary's, the small church near the landing-stage at the
southern end of the island, in the years before its
renovation in 1976. It had confessional boxes all along both
sides, and makeshift side-altars in between, with the pews

running right up against them. Going to confession there was a penitential exercise in itself. People were forever having to climb over others kneeling, there was a great crush and many faintings: for, each morning, hundreds had to queue there to make the confession that is an essential part of the second day of the station.[3]

It could also be any parish church from Heaney's childhood or mine. Echoes of the lovely metaphors of the Litany of Our Lady – 'House of Gold, pray for us; Ark of the Covenant, pray for us' – sound through the poem, part of the first word-music of a Catholic child. But it also recreates that close world of the examined and governed conscience, of the habit of self-arraignment that was instilled in that same susceptible imagination, and was required to be exercised formally from at least the age of seven – the 'age of the use of reason'.

That double mastery, of song and of guilt! At six, rehearsing for my First Confession, I was an expert in the categories of sin. The crippling 'scruples' of the Little Flower, Saint Thérèse of Lisieux, were to be envied, not avoided. In every thought, word and deed of my six-year-old day, I was already intimately involved in Christ's suffering and death – either sharing in its redemptive work, or collaborating with His torturers. And 'Father' would have to be told all about it, at least once a week.

Harry Williams writes in *The True Wilderness*:

The unquestioning acceptance of our own
blameworthiness, leading to confession and pardon,
possessed, for those who had experience of it,
something of the warmth and comfort of the nursery.
But our age has been sent away to school.[4]

Poem III of 'Station Island' is set in an ambiguous nursery, its rhymes a lovely liturgy, its authority paternal, its centre close and female, its child companion a ghost.

This is a childhood within doors, quite distinct from that

tactile world of mud and of dung in dark-clumped grass
that Heaney and Carleton between them evoked in the
second poem. And the farthest memories are of being very
small indeed – of the time when the child was able to enter
and inhabit 'the hold / of our big oak sideboard' – a sort of
'playing house'. Further and deeper in, peeling back layers
of tissue paper, the child is able to enter memories before
his own memory, the kept story of a life ended and grieved
for before his own even began.

The first ghost on the island is a name only, and that
name, 'a white bird trapped inside' the child in the
sideboard, is spoken about but is not uttered. Purgatory
does not grant her a voice or even a presence in the poem.
Elsewhere Heaney has told us[5] that the child is Agnes, his
father's sister, who died of TB in the 1920s. Within it, she
is one of the curiously unnamed females that haunt
Heaney's sequence with images of voiceless womanhood
and girlhood.

The nexus of images that is evoked by the child Agnes
is of an unrealised fertility, housed and dry, birds' eggs
held in the wreath of a nest. In a dream-like transition, a
cold draught lays beside it the image of another circle of
vegetation, damp and once more in Heaney's more familiar
outdoor world. This circle is inhabited not by arrested
possibility, but by absence. With a triplet that Heaney was
later to re-use almost verbatim (in the eighth sonnet of
'Clearances'[6]) about his mother's death, he introduces both
an incontrovertible exemplum of death's reality and the
possibility of resurgence:

> I thought of walking round
> and round a space utterly empty,
> utterly a source, like the idea of sound;
>
> like an absence stationed in the swamp-fed air
> above a ring of walked-down grass and rushes
> where we once found the bad carcass and scrags of hair
> of our dog that had disappeared weeks before.

'Utterly empty, utterly a source' – words that sound through the whole 'Station Island' sequence as the words of the Litany sound through this part of it. And with their utterance here the island and the pilgrimage almost disappear, become themselves an absence. Only the after-image of a circle of walked-down grass remains, the shimmer of a memory, perhaps, of doing the station early in the season, when the untrimmed spring grass around the 'beds' is gradually trodden down by the bare feet of the first batches of pilgrims.

Heaney's station on Station Island will continually slip through the fingers. The pilgrim is doing his station now and in the past, but the now is never quite as it should be, and the pilgrimages past side-slip into other pasts, till the shape of the whole becomes ever more clearly an iceberg of an autobiography – or, to Hibernise the image, the island we have landed on is really a great whale such as Saint Brendan beached on in the *Navigatio*,[7] the mainly submerged material of a life.

The structure of the station offers the pilgrim an outline of custom and rite, and repeated prayers that clear the mind like mantras or like sleep: specific memories swim up to the surface of consciousness. They will move Heaney's sequence almost imperceptibly from infancy to early childhood, and on soon to 'the shaky local voice of education'.

Now that he is on the island, the images of centring, of circling, begin. The cycle of rot and fertility that Carleton talked of on the straight and metalled mountain road foreshadowed it. Here it becomes physical and actual. From the circle of the clicking rosary beads in the second line right through to the circular tramplings of the dying dog, whether 'utterly empty' or 'utterly a source', the idea of the circuit that is at the heart of the Station Island pilgrimage is a sensuous presence, is made flesh for the first time. This remote and 'peasant' pilgrimage, with its stumps of beehive cells stumbled over by bare feet, has a share in the celestially inspired circling that was the architectonic principle for Dante's Purgatory.

But for the moment the shape of it is all that is suggested. The sunwise circuits of the saints' 'beds', with their possibility of spiralling on from one circle to the next, are not yet begun. Heaney the pilgrim is left with a small child's apprehension of deaths that haunt like a gramophone record with the needle stuck; memories laid down, perhaps, before speech. In the next poem the ghost he meets will not be lost for words, and he himself will, with some difficulty, become articulate. There will begin to be dialogue in his Purgatory.

First of all he, and I, must walk outside into the open air, and begin the real business of our first penitential station. We must begin our outdoor prayers with one Our Father, one Hail Mary, and one Creed, murmured as we kneel at the pathetic stump of Saint Patrick's cross – two crossed metal slats set in a fragment of carved stone column that was rescued from the 1632 razing. From there it is but a step to Saint Brigid's Cross where, with arms outstretched to the Donegal sky, we must utter the ancient words of renunciation: 'I renounce the World, the Flesh, and the Devil!' After this we will be released upon our circuits, first of the basilica, and then of the stone 'beds'.

I am suddenly horrified by the situation. Am I to make my station in all seriousness, and if not, why am I here? I walk across to the stone cross of Saint Brigid built into the basilica wall, and turn so that it is at my back. The four storeys of the men's hostel close off all view and sunlight. I am in their shadow. Pilgrims who have completed their mouthed renunciations move away and start on their beads; fresh ones join me at the wall. I know now that I cannot say these words, with all their skewed and gnostic impedimenta; so I tell the flickers of wind from the unseen lough that I *rejoice* in the world, and I *rejoice* in the flesh. Just for the moment, I leave out the devil.

The sweetness of belonging drains from my outstretched fingertips. I would rather be anywhere but here, at variance with so many. They genuflect on the flagstones round about me, then walk on out of this defile between the buildings, out to the next corner of the basilica, their heads braced into the north-west wind that blows off the lough. I follow, longing to be out of shelter and in earshot of the waves. The prescribed circuits of the building will bring me back four times to the relative calm of the piazza, but then will swing me out again, four times, to the lough's edge, almost to the wilds.

NOTES

1. *Traits & Stories*, 1876 edition, p.206.
2. Laurence J. Flynn, *Lough Derg*, p.[17].
3. Father Laurence J. Flynn told me of this major alteration in the conduct and siting of the station in a conversation during August 1987.
4. *The True Wilderness*, pp.144-5.
5. Neil Corcoran, *Seamus Heaney*, p.161.
6. In *The Haw Lantern*.
7. When the monks light a fire on what they think is an island, it starts into movement 'like a wave.' After their hasty escape, Brendan tells them not to be afraid. 'God revealed to me during the night in a vision the secret of this affair. Where we were was not an island, but a fish - the foremost of all that swim in the ocean. He is always trying to bring his tail to meet his head, but he cannot because of his length. His name is Jasconius.' *The Voyage of Saint Brendan* translated by John J. O'Meara, pp.18-19.

CHAPTER SIX

Raising the Kitchen Siege

Poem IV

2 August 1987: afternoon
  After Saint Brigid's Cross

The house I was bred in – ah, does it remain?
Low walls and loose thatch standing lone in the rain ...
Like the blackbird's left nest in the briar!

Padraic Colum, 'The Baltimore Exile'

A Mass Rock near Ardara, Co. Donegal

As I walk away from Saint Brigid's Cross, I half expect a thunderbolt to fall on me from God's medieval arsenal. I am lapsed. I am living in sin. I have not done my Easter – or any – duty for nearly twenty years. What has brought me to this heartland of my childhood faith is a spiritual curiosity in the widest sense, and not – I hope – any stirring of repentance for my long agnosticism. But the pilgrim-playing persona I have assumed is rudely confronted with these unregenerate medieval renunciations. I came impressed by the ritual's sheer survival through centuries. Now that I am required to articulate its words on the appointed place, I am far more than impressed – I am scared.

If I had renounced the flesh just now, would Michael then have been instantly lost to me? And surely I have already renounced quite enough of my world in coming to this crowded desert instead of to the wild coast of the Atlantic! I am not believer enough to knuckle under and say the words properly, nor – I am disturbed to discover – agnostic enough to regard them as meaningless. I am caught between meaning and meaning. The words of these renunciations are not words that 'slip, slide, perish, / Decay with imprecision.' They are hard and finished as crystals, ice fetters on my too fluid soul.

I had misgivings on the journey here, but this is the first moment at which I have really questioned my own sincerity in doing this pilgrimage. Heaney's old self-accusation, 'artful voyeur',[1] hits home to me as I stand where his imagined self stood three summers before. 'Once a Catholic, always a Catholic' goes the (Catholic) saying. Membership bestows a sort of lifelong passport that, even if never renewed, remains valid till one's (of course!) deathbed repentance: even mortal sin, in the old terminology, does not strip one of *this* nationality. And yet . . . I fear that I may have presumed too much on my old religion, and – worse – too much on my own self in coming here.

'... But all this you were clear of you walked into
over again. ...'

It is not Catholicism that has called me here, but poetry –
surely? But never have the two felt so uncomfortably
intertwined.

And now, too, I walk into the part of Heaney's sequence
that in past reading has made me feel ill at ease, the poems
in which the voices are those of men only, and the
developing story of a poet's 'seedtime' is one that is
peculiarly a boy's. Yet in these poems 'I will feel lost, /
Unhappy *and at home*',[2] for there is a particularly Irish
quality to their pattern of speaking men and silent women.

In Dante's *Purgatorio* and *Paradiso*, Beatrice is the
supreme guide and chider that even Virgil must give way
to. But on Heaney's island, the silence of all women and
girls is complete. They will figure, as they have done on the
pilgrimage journey, in brief, wordless parts: mild-mouthed
or lamenting, playing at houses or kitchen-bound;
glimpsed, back view only, through the keyhole of a keyhole
dress. Mothers, wives, lovers, they will appear and vanish
like upperworld ghosts. Only the men will be articulate
underworld shades, able to address their living visitant like
the inhabitants of Dante's *Commedia*, to voice their regrets,
their angers, the untold narratives left over from the
unfinished business of their lives. But haven't men always
been the articulate ones – or at least the heard and the
recorded ones – in Irish life and letters? And haven't the
women always been right behind them?

I walk on into the great circuit of the basilica walls. In
my own distress and doubt I keep in motion, knowing that
each time I pass and repass the starting-point at the south
corner the spirit of Heaney will still be hovering,
dumbstruck, like one of his own ghosts, at his half-
remembered Saint Brigid's cross.[3] It may be men only to
whom his island grants the privilege of speech, but that
privilege brings its own grim responsibilities, both for him
and for those whose spirits are conjured into his path and

sight; and for no man in so clear and agonising a form, perhaps, as the first man he meets.

*   *   *

For Heaney the pilgrim, the three Renunciations are 'dream words', and he is speechless altogether. He stands at the appointed place, with his arms outstretched in the ancient gesture of prayer, unable to utter them. He is fixed in the classic incapacity of nightmare, prevented even from enacting the circling motions of observance.

The anguished and disquieting voice of the first speaking soul of Purgatory breaks into his stasis and speechlessness. The soul's name, like that of the child in the previous poem, is spoken of but not given. Her name was a 'white bird trapped' withindoors; his rises 'wet and perished' from the ditch of memory. He is 'a young priest, glossy as a blackbird', and unlike her his whistle is wetted into speech.

The blackbird image rises out of the green world of the outdoors, and brings with it, briefly, a note from the world of early Irish nature poetry, and even, for a fleeting moment, an echo of King Sweeney's transformation.[4] But in a couple of words the priest has taken the listening pilgrim far from the grass and sod of Ireland, to the world of the foreign missions. For here is a boy who thought he had answered the highest call of community and faith, but found himself dying in utter spiritual and geographical dislocation.

He cries out from the far-flung mission fields; the distance from Ireland, however, is not as great as might appear. Such foreign parts have been always, and still are, far more present to the Irish imagination than to the English. Vast amounts of cash, per head, are donated in Ireland for the Third World; vast networks of missionary endeavour span the globe. Catholicism in its very name offers a universal frame of reference. The generosity of money and of person is fuelled by a deep sympathy between an historically oppressed peasantry and their oppressed contemporaries: the foreign mission field is the ultimate place to which a religious vocation calls Ireland's men and women. That it has enabled them to practise a subtler colonialism than that of the openly imperialist nations is another irony of Irish history.

The young priest may be glossy as a blackbird, but he is limed by vocation from early adolescence. He rises up from memory, a childhood neighbour who took the path through his education that the future poet carefully avoided: Greek as well as Latin, junior seminary in his teens. He may have thought the World, the Flesh and the Devil had been summarily and finally identified – and dismissed? – by his priestly vows of Poverty, Chastity and Obedience. But the living of those vows has mired him in complexities he was ill-prepared for.

The World, the Flesh, and the Devil . . . The World he looks back on from the world of the dead is utterly foreign, utterly beyond the reach of his Catholicism. The Flesh that still confronts him in the rain-forest of his purgatory is 'bare-breasted / women and rat-ribbed men'. The Devil is a horror in the 'abandoned mission compound' that echoes the nameless horror that sent Kurtz mad in *Heart of Darkness*. And in that pagan setting his vocation, the calling that was meant to give shape and meaning to his life, has become merely 'a steam off drenched creepers'.

This very first of the island's speaking ghosts opens a door into the dark. For late twentieth century Heaney there is no vision of the bliss of the saved to offer to a believing readership, no authoritative voice 'from the other side':

'... The god has, as they say, withdrawn. ...'

The priest's stuttered eloquence conveys something of the sense of risk and fear in medieval accounts of the Lough Derg experience, but none of the solid certainties of the medieval faith. It is as though the polar certainties of Hell and Heaven have fallen away along with the god, and the living and the dead share the same state of becoming and of pain. Heaney the pilgrim can himself only achieve fluency when he stops trying to speak his own Renunciations, and gently calls the priest back to the Ireland of their childhood. For the priest is stuck in his own nightmare too, circling again and again like a caged beast on the place of his pain, instead of spiralling sunwise into acceptance and understanding.

Ironically, the very pictures Heaney offers him of his summer vacations from the seminary lead them both into the breeding-ground of that nightmare, the cosy and apparently wholesome round of farm kitchens and home-made bread. For the Irish priesthood has in the past tended to flourish in an enclosure of sacrifice and connivance in which women and men made the matching wards and levers of a locked pattern. Between them they created and maintained the religious patriarchy that still dominates areas of home and state – and sexuality – in Ireland. Within it, the sacrifices of the women are made meaningful by their enabling of their sons. And that mother–son relationship is often – still – a fiercer passion than anything felt for a husband. From the mid-nineteenth century onwards – since the drastic drop in the population caused by the Famine altered so many of the old social patterns – Irish fathers tended, in the country areas especially, to be far older than their wives. The resemblance to the traditional picture of the 'Holy Family' – three virgins of three generations bound together by the say-so of an asexual angel – is uncomfortably close. It effectively sublimates or diverts sexuality for all involved.[5]

And how the priesthood have been petted in conservative Ireland! Not just their mothers, but all women who have kept alive in their hearts the sacred home-making ideals that De Valera enshrined in the 1937 Constitution,[6] would fall over themselves to serve a priest:

'... Something in them would be ratified
when they saw you at the door in your black suit,
arriving like some sort of holy mascot.

You gave too much relief, you raised a siege
the world had laid against their kitchen grottoes
hung with holy pictures and crucifixes.'

This boy had answered what was, in the eyes of his
community, the supreme call, 'unaware / that what [he]
thought was chosen was convention'. He was 'doomed to
the decent thing', doomed to play his ordained part in the
most heartfelt and Marian sacrifice an Irish family can
make: to offer up its son to the Lord's service, as Mary and
Joseph offered the twelve-year-old Christ at the Temple,
and as later Mary on her own accepted even the horror of
Golgotha for him.

*   *   *

I keep thinking of the religious in my own Irish family. Of
my mother's beloved cousin Tony Dwyer, who went out to
the rainforests of Burma fresh from his ordaining, and died
of blackwater fever after a mere six weeks in the mission
field. And – more happily – of my uncle, her brother, who
walked out of junior seminary, refusing to go on into
orders, and went back all the way home to east Galway,
leaving his glossy black suit behind him. He it was who
later fell in love at Lough Derg. Our family wasn't very
successful when it came to the priesthood, much to my
grandmother's sorrow.

It was the nuns, the women religious, who were more
central in every way to my childhood. There were my two
eldest aunts, who had been promised to the convent by my
grandmother from babyhood – a bargain she had made
with Christ in return for bearing a son[7] – and who went

there without question: 'Wasn't I indentured to the religious life?' says my surviving aunt, nearly eighty now. Then, a generation later, there was my own very favourite cousin, who chose to enter an order that, in return for her self, gave her a finer higher education than any secular choice her family could have afforded. She came close to death in the mission fields of Mali, and has had to learn, in the painful disablement that that illness has left her with, a radically new interpretation of the call she hears from Christ.

What of all the other nuns, though, the early mentors of my soul – those who schooled me in both 'modesty' and scholasticism from the age of four? In their centuries-out-of-date clothes they fostered passivity, service, silence. Shyly proud, they commended their own vocation as an Irish girl's highest calling. Saint Paul's 'better to marry than burn' was quietly conceded, but as a poor second best to the religious life. They seem, in my memory, to have been afraid even of accidental touching, to have kept constant custody of their hands and eyes under the generous eaves and overlaps of their habits. When I was at boarding-school, we girls all devoutly believed that the nuns wore shifts that covered them completely at all times, and especially when they were in the bath. The sight even of their own bodies naked was to be avoided.

After years out of touch with convent life, years of being lapsed and disconnected from Catholicism, I have recently found myself visiting and talking with nuns again. It is all part, of course, of returning to Ireland. Since my first long drive 'home' in 1980 – across England, Wales, and Ireland's midlands to the far west, in search of that wild solitude – I have inevitably been welcomed back to the capacious heart of my Irish family as well. There is such kindness there, such unquestioning hospitality – and from 'sisters', too, who are no blood relations.

I have sat up late for *The Late, Late Show* with my aunt and her pals in a modest house in Galway City, eating our way with no thought of abstinence through a big box of chocolates. Lent had, after all, recently come to an end. The whole of Ireland seemed one family that night: every person or name that appeared on the programme – even every winner of Gay Byrne's cash draw – was known to someone in that small room. I have stayed with my cousin's community in Paris, drinking wine from the Order's own vineyard in relaxed mixed company as they recover from a day's tough teaching. In their networks of mutual support, in their radical and international viewpoint, they have at times seemed the most creatively feminist 'household' I know. The Galway nuns had spent *their* day in some of that city's most harrowing and necessary social work. In both houses, the medieval habits, in the sense of attitudes as well as of clothing, that I remember from my childhood are discarded by all but the eldest. These 1980s nuns are not set apart from the laity by their clothing, or even by their field of work. Is their vocation something extra given to them, rather than something renounced?

Above all, I have hugged and been hugged by today's nuns. I have seen and felt the warm and loving and physically grounded support they offer each other now. It is a support that grows out of the inclusion of sexuality rather than its denial. And I have learnt of the breaking of silence, too; that some of these women with the freedom of their single state have become agents and actors of radical change – and not just in the field of religion.

I lapsed from Catholicism in the summer of 1968, as did so many. The invasion of Czechoslovakia made an emotional but unquestioned connection for me. The unleashing of that brute authoritarianism on the streets of Prague seemed to be part of the same world as Pope Paul VI's 'infallible' encyclical of that summer, ironically called *Humanae Vitae*: 'Of Human Life'. It seemed that all the warmth and light of the Prague spring and of the Second Vatican Council were being finally extinguished at the same moment by the old patriarchies. 'Daddy, Daddy, I'm through,' I cried, and walked out of the whole Catholic thing.

And now I have walked into it 'over again'. Here I am on Station Island. Have I walked into the worn ruts of the past or into a fresh and fructifying furrow? Is there a place for me in this communion, even on a temporary basis? The three Renunciations have come too early in the proceedings, for me as well as for Heaney.

*   *   *

I keep on walking round the walls of the basilica, eager for a view of the lough, for openness, but find it grim when I reach it. Dull sky and grey lake waters. A sudden damp wind that cuts coldly through the gaps in clothes. Two or three tiny pale dots of houses only, and they scattered far from each other on the bleak slopes of the northern hills.

I have felt utterly estranged from my fellow pilgrims at Saint Brigid's cross. Now the landscape before me can offer nothing to rejoice body or spirit. And yet, as I slowly pace the round of the basilica, I have to recognise that this place is a cradle of safety, a haven of unquestioned belonging for the unquestioning – and even, perhaps, for the doubting. A Catholic from the North, even a lapsed and blasphemous one like myself, breathes an air of freedom at Lough Derg that those from the twenty-six counties can only guess at the need for. The 'tight gag of place' that works on Catholics who grow up north of the Border loosens as they cross into the south. It is so real, so instinctive a self-custody that even in England, and even after twenty years away, I find myself cautious, even silent, in the company of Northern Irish Protestants. I realise that, approaching Lough Derg from the South, I had only had a taste of the meaning of that border crossing as we drove briefly into and out of the North. I had disremembered the precise colour of that freedom.

Hundreds of my fellow pilgrims, it seems, are from the

North's beleaguered minority. I hear the vowels of Ulster
low and musical about me, the murmurings of innumerable
Hail Maries in the accents I grew up with. The easy
emotions of the bus journey seem shallow now compared
to the stirrings that begin in this aural embrace. The boat
has carried us all – and especially the Northerners – into
the heartland of Irish spirituality, and suddenly it is the
norm for us to be Catholic. It is not only geographical
proximity that makes the Northern tradition of coming to
do the Station so very strong.

All sorts and conditions of men and women walk with
me, slowly, each of us preoccupied with our beads, each of
us finding our own speed as unaccustomed feet spread on
the cold slabs. Here, in the physical walking of the Station,
the patheticness and egality of bare feet take me by
surprise. I had not anticipated their gift of fellowship. No
pomposity of manner or dress can survive the nakedness of
these extremities. Age, gender, status are of no account.
There are even priests and nuns as barefoot as the rest. Our
feet are our balancing points, our newly felt contact with
the ground.

Our eyes are cast downwards in reverence, and to watch
out for excruciating points of stray gravel. Mine are drawn
to the incongruity of bare feet appearing beneath coats and
woollies and trousers as we shiver in the wind off the
lough. I think of Liz Lochhead's beggar surprising a girl
into first tears over the end of a relationship:

> It was just his poor
> pink and purple naked foot
> out on a limb
> exposed.[8]

I ponder the ritual of Maundy Thursday, with its traditional
message of humility and service on the part of Christ or
monarch. Perhaps those who offer their naked feet for
washing are as cleansed of vanity as the one who washes
them? Intent on the task of saying seven decades of the

rosary, we walk on cautiously, stripped down and equal before each other, on poor, unaccommodated feet. This is the territory of Antaeus – the Titan whose story frames Part I of Heaney's *North*. Our feet are 'mould-hugger[s]';[9] skin to stone, they 'cannot be weaned / Off the earth's long contour'.[10] Their movement is the most ancient and essential locomotion practised by mankind. Somehow, the double connection of the blackbird-priest with bicycles – his name 'like an old bicycle wheel in a ditch', and the pilgrim's surprised 'I could only see you on a bicycle' – makes him seem more remote than ever from this pedestrian pilgrimage. Even Heaney, for heaven's sake, has forsaken his wheels for the moment . . .

Out here between the basilica and the lough, though we have flagstones and tarmac under our feet, and no soil or living grass, we are out of the kitchen siege and into open air. And as I walk with the others, the slow consonance of all our small steps reconciles me to my part in this pilgrimage. Despite the showy episode of the Renunciations at the start, it is now made up of minute elements of mumbled, undramatic sameness: Hail Maries, Hail Maries, Hail Maries, and here and there an Our Father and an Apostles' Creed. The kindness of the island touches me. I remember Sean O'Faolain's description of it as 'a brief, harsh Utopia of equality in nakedness'.[11]

NOTES

1. 'Punishment' in *North*.
2. 'The Tollund Man' in *Wintering Out* – italics mine.
3. Lough Derg pilgrims will know that 'the stone pillar and the iron cross' belong to Saint Patrick, and to the previous stage in the devotion. Saint Brigid's Cross is

   A fragment of the Middle Ages set
   Into the modern masonry of the conventional Basilica ...

   (*Lough Derg*, Patrick Kavanagh).

4. See the much-translated early lyric 'The Lagan Blackbird'.
Heaney's translation is printed in *Preoccupations*, p.181.
5. See Hugh Brody's *Inishkillane*, p.110 and *passim*; also Patrick
Kavanagh's long poem 'The Great Hunger'.
6. Eamonn de Valera – the one leader of the 1916 Easter Rising
who refused to have any women involved in his part of the
action – wanted 'an Ireland "whose countryside would be bright
with cosy homesteads, whose villages would be joyous with the
romping of sturdy children, the contests of athletic youths, the
laughter of comely maidens". Now as president, he took the
opportunity to ensure that women, whether they liked it or not,
would give priority to their duties as wives and mothers.'
(Margaret Ward, *Unmanageable Revolutionaries*, p.238.) His draft
constitution contained the following clauses, which were strongly
objected to at the time:

Article 40
1   All citizens shall, as human persons, be held equal
before the law. This shall not be held to mean that the State
shall not in its enactments have due regard to differences of
capacity, physical and moral, and of social function.

Article 41
2-1   In particular, the State recognises that by her life
within the home, a woman gives to the State a support
without which the common good cannot be achieved.
2-2   The State shall, therefore, endeavour to ensure that
mothers shall not be obliged by economic necessity to
engage in labours to the neglect of their duties in the home.

Article 45
4-2   The State shall endeavour to ensure that the
inadequate strength of women and the tender age of
children shall not be abused, and that women and children
shall not be forced by economic necessity to enter
avocations unsuited to their sex, age or strength.

The Women Graduates Association and the Joint Committee of
Women's Societies and Social Workers campaigned to have these
clauses deleted, and to retain 'Section 3 of the 1922 Constitution,
which simply and unequivocally stated that everyone over the
age of 21 who qualified as an Irish citizen was, without

distinction of sex, to be accorded that right.' (Margaret Ward, op. cit., p.239.)

7.   See 'She promises her firstborn daughters to the religious life if God will allow her to survive a dangerous miscarriage' in the 'Galway' section of the author's *Settlements*.

8.   'Poem for other Poor Fools', in *Dreaming Frankenstein*.

9.   'Hercules and Antaeus'.

10.   'Antaeus'.

11.   'Lovers of the Lake', in the Collected Short Stories Vol. 2, *The Heat of the Sun*, p.35.

CHAPTER SEVEN

The Cistern Contains:
The Fountain Overflows

Poem V

2 August 1987: late afternoon
  Round the basilica and on to the 'beds'

Father Mat came slowly walking, stopping to
Stare through gaps at ancient Ireland sweeping
In again with all its unbaptized beauty:
The calm evening,
The whitethorn blossoms,
The smell from ditches that were not Christian.

Patrick Kavanagh, 'Father Mat'

Saint Patrick describing the cave at Lough Derg,
after a woodcut in Peter de Navalibus' *Catalogue of Saints*

At the end of Poem IV, the shade of the priest disappears with the suddenness of dream. A mist rises, no longer 'a steam off drenched creepers', but 'the first breath of spring' smoking up from the drizzly roads of home. Heaney the pilgrim is released from stasis into the motion of wading, and then, at the beginning of Poem V, into a more specific rural rhythm: he falls in behind another pilgrim, like one 'lifting swathes at a mower's heels'.

Behind the basilica, there is more congenial company awaiting him than the anguished priest with his awkward questions about religious faith. The pilgrim walks into the world of letters and poetry, and into a male fellowship and fosterage that is instinct once more with the natural – and outdoor – world.

The first fosterer, Master Murphy of Anahorish School, greets his old pupil with an easy recognition – 'Good man, / good man yourself' – and his feet are eloquently bare. The polished shoes of the young missionary priest, rooted to the one place and 'unexpectedly secular', seem, in retrospect, more than ever a sign that he, as much as his God, has withdrawn from both community and faith. He had travelled far from Ireland in the service of his religion, but even though there is no doubt about Master Murphy's deep rootedness in a very particular Derry place, Anahorish, it is the schoolteacher who is in spirit and practice more truly in touch than he is with 'abroad'.

For, as the lettered man in a rural parish – the 'Master'– Murphy is the one who can unlock the coded voices of distant emigrants for their unlettered relatives at home: he is reader and writer of their rustling letters. He has the skill, too, to introduce the boy Heaney to the metaphorical world of 'letters' – a world that spans centuries as well as oceans. Knowledge of Latin in particular has linked Ireland, from its first flowering as the Island of Saints and Scholars, with the culture of all Europe.

There is a growing sense of certainty, a strengthening of spring, in this meeting with Master Murphy, the country boy's first initiator into that 'sweet equal republic' of letters.

Earlier in the sequence, grass and the 'tender bladed
growth' of corn were walked down, slushed through. Here
there are persistent images of mowing and scything. Even
the grass that has now grown over the site of Anahorish
School is grazed by dairy herds. Does the shade of Brigid,
the saint-cum-goddess of dairying, shimmer faintly over it?

The greening of Heaney's first school is the only
message from the dead that Master Murphy can bring to
speech. But there is no grim 'Death the Reaper' shadow in
any of these images of cut or cropped grass. Anahorish
School has been overgrown, but that, like the mowing, is
part of a rural rhythm of fall and regeneration that has no
trace of morbidity. This springtime has the feel of the May
mornings of medieval love lyrics, and the sensuality of the
real countryside:

> Morning field smells came past on the wind,
> the sex-cut of sweetbriar after rain,
> new-mown meadow hay ...

'Declensions sang on air like a *hosanna*'.[1] The chant of
'*Mensa, mensa, mensam*' takes the 'table' it signifies out of
the close kitchen and plants it in the green outdoors. It is as
though Heaney himself had literally been to a
'hedge-school', had lived at the time when Latin was taught
(illegally) to the Irish peasantry in the open air;[2] or when
the Latin words of the Mass were said over the improvised
table of a Mass-rock, out in the boglands remote from
hostile scrutiny.

Mass-rock? No, nothing so simply Christian. For the
pilgrim Heaney has not only skipped his renunciations;
now, having turned round to greet his old master, he is
'faced wrong way' against the flow of the other pilgrims.
The Latin words sing 'in the air like a busy whetstone', and
the strange image suddenly takes me to the pagan world
that Sir Gawain, the knight with a special devotion to Mary,
brushes with towards the end of the late medieval poem *Sir
Gawain and the Green Knight*. While he waits by the Green

Chapel, the knight hears a noise 'As one upon a gryndelston hade grounden a sythe'.[3] The Green Chapel itself, a grassy mound that is all hollow within, 'nobot an olde cave', has an uncanny resemblance to Saint Patrick's cave or 'pitte' in the medieval accounts of the Purgatory of Station Island.

The overgrown oratory that Gawain, the uptight knight of 'courtesye' and convention, has found in the wilderness is the Green Man's chapel, a place of pagan – or, as Gawain would have it, devilish – ceremony. (Wait! Is that a gull swooping in low from the lough, or is it the spirit of King Sweeney himself brushing the air of the Purgatory . . . ?) It was, after all, a 'devil' who wrote the 'Proverbs of Hell' in Blake's 'Memorable Fancy',[4] and lamented the passing of natural religion into the structures of abstraction and institutions:

> The ancient Poets animated all sensible objects with Gods or Geniuses, calling them by the names and adorning them with the properties of woods, rivers, mountains, lakes ...
> Till a system was formed, which some took advantage of, & enslav'd the vulgar by attempting to realize or abstract the mental deities from their objects: thus began Priesthood; ...
> Thus men forgot that All deities reside in the human breast.

The pilgrim is far from the exercise others are absorbed in, far from the letter of the island's devotions. When a second master speaks suddenly, unnannounced, and offers love as *the great / moving power and spring of verse*, it is a love that (despite the phrase's origin in Father Gerard Manley Hopkins' notebooks) is not here delimited by any specifically Christian connotation. It is simply *'Feeling, and / in particular, love'*. And what sharp and sensuous feeling!

I drank three cups of water from the well.

It was very cold. It stung me in the ears.

This Helicon is actual and used, a farm-well at Toome just
down the road from the Heaneys' farm; it is also, like the
wells of Heaney's early poem 'Personal Helicon', a direct
and living link with ancient belief in the sacredness of
springs, and their connection with poetry. This second
fosterer unequivocally declares poetry itself to be a sacred
calling – but one that comes with the no-nonsense force of
a box to the ears. He delivers himself of his aphorisms and
is gone, uninterrogated, barely described – leaving his old
pupil to the jibes of an actual practitioner of the art: Patrick
Kavanagh,

> a third fosterer,
> slack-shouldered and clear-eyed: 'Sure I might have
>   known
> once I had made the pad, you'd be after me
> sooner or later. Forty-two years on
> and you've got no farther ...'

                        *   *   *

1942, 1984:[5] Heaney the pilgrim facing wrong way into the
flow of pilgrims, Kavanagh observing them wryly from an
ambivalent vantage point . . . How this island draws its
country's writers in this century of doubt! The ghost of
Sean O'Faolain flutters somewhere near the edge of vision,
keeping a compassionate eye on his 'lovers of the lake'.
Denis Devlin is about, too, mixing the heavy impasto for
his mystic poem 'Lough Derg'. But as I complete at last my
fourth circuit of the basilica, and walk out across the
amazingly soft and threaded lawn before it, it's the cheek
of the Monaghan poet that I am in need of to lighten my
heart.

I am in the sheltered centre of the island now, facing the

slope that holds the ancient stone 'beds'. I raise my eyes to the highest point on the grassed mound that lies beyond them, and summon up my own pilgrimage ghost: Patrick Kavanagh taking his ease there, right on top of where the ancient cave is supposed to have been. He takes a packet of sandwiches out of his rucksack, and starts on the serious business of eating whilst all around him fast. Now and then he throws a crust towards the fasting pilgrims as they toil round the cramped bed of Saint Brigid just below him. A future Prior is shaking with fury down on the path by the men's hostel: 'Monsignor Flood had no time at all for Kavanagh after *that* performance'.[6] But, in *Lough Derg*,

> The poet wrote it down as best he knew ...
> He too was one of them.

As I stand in the long queue waiting for my turn on the beds, I need the social inclusiveness of Kavanagh's sequence to temper the introspection of Heaney's. Although his conduct as pilgrim was unconventional (and made him liable to instant deportation, according to my rule-sheet), as writer he offers me a waking and peopled Lough Derg like the one I see before me in 1987, for his 'Communion of Saints / Is a Communion of Individuals'. There are shopkeepers, farmers, girls of Donegal –

> Wives whose husbands have angina pectoris,
> Wives whose husbands have taken to drinking . . .
>   A Leitrim man
> With a face as sad as a flooded hay-field,
> Leaned in an angle of the walls with his rosary beads
>   in his hands.

Here is a 'felde ful of folke' from which many individual voices rise up in the course of his poem: and the women speak too, whether in prayer of 'banal beggary', or in words 'as integral and completed as the emotion / Of men and women cloaking a burning emotion / In the rags of the commonplace'. Kavanagh's distinctive mix of satire and compassion includes all the faithful.

On my August afternoon there are so many pilgrims on the island that we must queue in lines of six at the bottom of the stony slope, waiting our turn to begin the intricate circuits of its ruined cells. Their low walls cluster on the steep slope like ancient hut circles, and between the highest three – those of Saints Brigid, Brendan and Catherine – the naked and slant-bedded schist juts through the scanty grass. On this very place Kavanagh saw the history of a whole community as well as of its individuals:

> The middle of the island looked like the memory
> Of some village evicted by the Famine,
> Some corner of a field beside a well
> Old stumps of walls where a stunted boor-tree is
> > growing.
> These were the holy cells of saintly men –
> O that was the place where Mickey Fehan lived
> And the Reillys before they went to America in the
> > Fifties.
> No, this is Lough Derg in county Donegal –
> So much alike is our historical
> And spiritual pattern, a heap
> Of stones anywhere is consecrated
> By love's terrible need.

It is a love that makes whole the random dismantlings of history, akin to the love that is the 'moving power' of poetry itself.

And now I have reached the front row of the queue. The young ushers motion us on to the penitential beds. Six of us climb up the gravelly steep path to the farthest cell and begin the most ancient part of the station.

At the Bed
  a) walk three times around the outside, by your
  right hand, while saying three 'Our Fathers', three

'Hail Marys' and one 'Creed';
b) kneel at the entrance to the Bed and repeat these prayers;
c) walk three times around the inside and say these prayers again;
d) kneel at the cross in the centre and say these prayers for the fourth time.

The most difficult task of all is to stay upright on the slippery schist, and to all fit on to the very limited space. No wonder we are only allowed to start in staggered groups of six! The foot-high circle of stone wall round Saint Brigid's bed is tiny. Processing round the outside is not so bad, except that the bare rock falls away steeply at one side, and is well polished by the continual passage of feet. The inside circuit is crowded even when there are only three of us 'walking' round it, since at least two other pilgrims are kneeling at the plain iron cross in the centre. We inch our way round and over them. Very soon I realise that it will not, as I feared, be my feet that will suffer from this pilgrimage, unless I cut them on a sharp stone: already it is my knees that are raw from the tops of the stone walls, and from the gravelly ground. And I have just begun. How calloused and tough my knees were during the distant years of my believing. How soft and unused they are now.

Unfit, unfit. But how shall I justify my being on this island at all unless I at least carry out the letter of the station? Michael, lapsed Anglican, could not stomach coming with me to do it on those terms. I thought, and still think, despite those Renunciations at the start of the station, that I can. How we keep the reflexes of lives we think we have shed! And I am confirmed into continuing by the last thing I had imagined before I came. Somehow, in the face of all the accounts I read and heard of the hundreds who crowd on to the island on each day of the pilgrimage season, I always pictured myself doing this particular part of the station in solitude. Now the welcome warmth of other people presses about me, and arms reach towards me with easy intimacy, either to save or be saved from falling on to harsh stone.

When I look about me I see some of my companions from the bus journey above and below me on the penitential slope. The overweight woman has cast aside her four-inch stilettoes, and is slowly negotiating one of the larger beds further down. She has a beatific smile on her face. Does she know that her left foot is leaving a blot of blood on the stones at every step?[7] The rugger hero is transformed by his eyes-shut devoutness as he kneels at one of the crosses. The Mills and Boon readers are over on Saint Columba's bed, looking now like young women instead of teenagers. Is it the serene, serious expressions on their clear faces? What is this peace that has worked its visible change on everyone? Perhaps they are already receiving the gift of the island that Sean O'Faolain speaks of, 'its sense of remoteness from the world, almost a sensation of the world's death. It is the source of the island's kindness. Nobody is just matter, poor to be exploited by rich, weak to be exploited by the strong; in mutual generosity each recognises the other only as a form of soul.'[8]

'... almost a sensation of the world's death.' I remember how the rite of baptism in the early Celtic church enacted a sort of death for the catechumen: how he or she took salt upon the tongue, and had the chrism of death's anointing spilt on the water's surface before immersion. And I remember how in the fourteenth century the ritual of Saint Patrick's Purgatory required all the worldly paraphernalia of death – wills, coffins and mock funerals – in order to prepare the minds and hearts of those who would enter its fearsome black cave. Up to the eighteenth century pilgrims had the Requiem Mass said for them before entering the cave.[9]

That cave's lost site lies somewhere under this small hill behind me. I am facing east now, looking out over the lake again, my last circuits of the largest penitential bed completed. I stand for a moment at the water's edge, then wade in a little to kneel on one of the stones that was part, it is said, of the old Purgatory that was dismantled and hurled into the lake in 1632. There are still more prayers to be said. And I realise that *this* is the moment that Heaney evokes in 'Triptych':

> Everything in me
> Wanted to bow down, to offer up,
> To go barefoot, foetal and penitential,
>
> And pray at the water's edge.[10]

The prayer 'at the water's edge' is the single expansive moment of solitude in this processional devotion, otherwise so crowded and communal. The sensual slop of water round my feet, and the unpeopled view out over a gentle reedy inlet of the lake towards two wooded islets, set it apart as the one contemplative window in the conduct of the station. How strange to be my own self again, with the wave cry, the wind cry. And do I now accept the 'offer it up' that I turned away from in January with such distaste? Have I done what my Irish female relatives pray for on my behalf in their nightly 'intentions'? Have I returned to Mother Church, to her – in the words of the baptismal liturgy – 'spotless womb of the divine spring'?

Hurry, hurry. The basilica bell is calling us to Mass, and I must complete my station quickly with three brief prayers under Saint Patrick's iron cross, and then go in with everyone else for the day's chief ritual: the supper and sacrifice of the Lord.

NOTES

1. 'Alphabets', II, in *The Haw Lantern*.
2. See the play *Translations* by Brian Friel, and William Carleton's essay 'The Hedge School' in *Traits and Stories*.
3. *Sir Gawain and the Green Knight*, 1.2202.

4.   *The Marriage of Heaven and Hell*, plate 6 et seq.

5.   There is a curious feature to the confident giving of years and year-counts within the text. Kavanagh's poem has an unequivocal internal date, 1942. This passage in Heaney's response to it suggests a date for *his* poem, and his imagined pilgrimage, of 1984: forty-two plus forty-two. However, *Station Island* was published in that very year, and the notes to the completed text are dated February 1984, months before the earliest date on which the (real) pilgrimage of that year could have been undertaken.

6.   A story related to the author by Father Laurence J. Flynn in 1987.

7.   The thought that someone might contract hepatitis B, or even HIV, from walking barefoot in the bloody tracks of others did not occur to me while on the island. On the contrary, before I arrived on the Purgatory, I had heard much of its vaunted healthiness. But when I said to a fellow pilgrim later that day that it was wonderful that no one ever injured themselves, or went down with pneumonia as a result of their devotions, she laughed briefly and then shook her head in some seriousness: 'Wasn't I here just last summer with one of the Sisters from our parish, and didn't she slip just below Saint Brigid's Bed and do such harm to her back that she's never walked since?'

8.   Sean O'Faolain, *Lovers of the Lake*, p.35.

9.   See the *Lough Derg Guide* by Joseph Duffy, p.17.

10.   'Triptych III', in *Fieldwork*.

CHAPTER EIGHT

Translated and Given

Poem VI

2 August 1987: 6 p.m.
    The Mass of the first day

                          Lovers will find
A hedge-school for themselves and learn by heart
All that the clergy banish from the mind
When hands are joined and the head bows in the dark.

                           Austin Clarke, 'Penal Law'

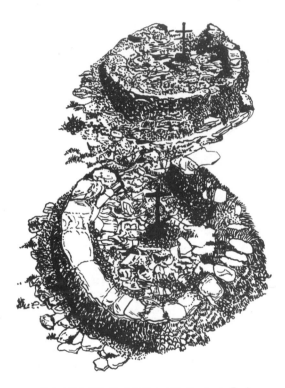

Saint Brigid's Bed & Saint Catherine's Bed

The church is full. We shuffle up together on the long pews to make space as more and more pilgrims enter in answer to the bell. The chaste interior is green with an underwatery light. As the last-comers squeeze in, a cheerful company of celebrants and servers strides with light step on to the sanctuary floor. They smile us welcome, give us a feeling of festival, of holyday. There is an instant rustle of relaxation throughout the gathering.

I think I can breathe in this atmosphere of . . . I strain for the word. Is it 'fellowship'? Informality? This ritual, surely, will be different, will have moved away from the unregenerate world of the Renunciations? The old liturgy begins: 'I will go unto the altar of God'. A thousand people answer: 'To God who has gladdened my youth.' Even now that it is Englished, it is utterly familiar. Long ago, in *my* glad youth, I knelt at a prie-dieu, a single voice calling out these responses – though in Latin then – for a whole congregation. At my convent boarding-school there were no boys to serve at the weekday Masses; the priest had to make do with girls.

But the memory troubles me. Because we were female, those of us singled out for this 'honour' could not walk our part, or dress up in the boys' cassocks and lace. Kept out of the sanctuary, railed off from the act, we had to serve with a disembodied voice. Is it different now that all of us, men and women, speak the responses together? But on Station Island there are still only men in possession of the sanctuary – the place that counts. Does it help that they smile?

I am transported away from awkward query, and into wonder, for now we sit back to listen to the scriptures, and the readings that we have chanced on in the Church's calendar take us to desert places, and then, in the Gospel, to a lake. Listen. Here are the Israelites receiving manna to ward off starvation in the wilderness. Here is Peter walking, for a few moments, on the waters of Galilee. And here *we* are, fasting, with one wretched 'Lough Derg meal' of dry toast and black tea to look forward to; and, like Peter on Galilee's freshwater 'sea', we have 'come over the waters' in answer to a summoning. What strange serendipity in the calendar's disposition has given me a Proper of the Mass so appropriate to being on Lough Derg?

Galilee . . . I am transported by the Gospel words in particular, and by Lake Galilee's self, or the pictures of it that swim up from the summer of sixty-eight, when I and the fellow student I'd married the year before sought out that northern part of 'the Holy Land' at a turning-point in our faith. For we were both cradle Catholics, Ken from the English tradition and I from the Irish, but both utterly committed to the radical and deeply humane reforms begun by Pope John XXIII. This was proving the most difficult year yet under the hostile rule of his successor.

So, while many of our contemporaries were caught up in the quite different conflicts and campaigns of that summer, Ken and I went back to the very ground of Christ's humanity: 'Palestine'. I remember us going up to our necks in the luke-warm waters of Galilee's lake, walking knee-deep in the dust of its hot tracks. I remember touching the throats of quernstones in the ruins of Capernaum, hearing a snake in the dry cistus where Herod's palace once lay on the lake's south-east shore, watching pied kingfishers quarter the lake like sea-swallows – and saying to each other, 'Christ must have known these things.' His physical and material life felt very close, the plainness of his words most true. Why not keep the Sermon on the Mount as 'gospel', we said, and let the professionals who came after him – especially Paul – go hang?

The whole edifice of the institution that had been built over his life began to slip and melt for us there, like the dissolving church of Van Gogh's late painting, 'L'Église d'Auvers-sur-Oise'. It was later, and further south, on the ancient footpath from Bethany to Jerusalem, that it slid away for good.

We were walking westwards, out of night. The swift dawn of those latitudes was soaring up behind us from the

desert hills of Judaea, but the walls of the old city before us
were still a tawny grey. Then the gilded domes of its
embattled faiths, and sects of faiths, caught the first rays:
the Dome of the Rock, the El Aqsa Mosque. It was not just
Catholicism's dust I was shaking off my sandals. Slowly,
perceptibly, the wide level of pre-dawn's grey pool of
half-light drained down into the Hebron valley, and the
stones of the city walls – ramparts first, then bastions, then
the very rock they were rooted in – became as golden as
the domes. I sat amongst the olive trees of Gethsemane,
weeping and rejoicing to be free, and Ken laid his hands
tenderly on the bark of one of them. It had, perhaps, been
a sapling in Christ's day. We were at one with the Christ
who had angrily cleared the precincts of the Temple two
millennia earlier; but, cleared or no, we didn't want to
worship in any house or institution of his Father ever again.
We found ourselves well outside the city of God, in the
clear bright air of morning.

Strange that in those days of change and protest –
religious, secular, political – neither I, nor anyone I then
knew or read, queried the near-invisibility of women in the
campaigns that we were all, both men and women,
involved in. Within our own married life, I and Ken were,
of course, intending to be equals. In the outside world it
was the power of hierarchies, not patriarchies in particular,
that we were all kicking against. There was an absence
there, both within the campaigns and in their intent, that
only becomes apparent in retrospect. Was that the
beginning of the flaw in our marriage of supposed equals?
We, and so many of our friends and contemporaries who
married in the 'old dispensation', eventually found our
marriages breaking down when we experimented, in all
innocence, with the new insights of the seventies and
eighties.

My way into those insights was poetry, and not initially
the poetry of women. That came later, and in confirming
abundance. All through the exhausting years of caring for
small children, it was in Heaney's successive volumes –

Death of a Naturalist, Door into the Dark, Wintering Out – that
I found essential nourishment: they told me where I came
from, so that I could begin to remember who I was. Their
voice was my half-forgotten vernacular, their roots were
deep in the female elements of water and land. He seemed
something rare amongst contemporary poets – a man who
spoke out of the feminine in himself. His words were a
small but valued part of my long and slow subversion.

This Mass is in another vernacular altogether. I wake up
to the bland English that has taken the place of Latin. Is it
because I am comparatively unfamiliar with the liturgy in
English that its clear male message hits home so hard to me
now, on Station Island? My memories of the waters of
Galilee may have distracted me at first, but as the Mass
continues to its ancient and essential climax, the
consecration of the bread and the wine, a slow anger rises
up in me. The green light of the basilica thickens to grey. In
this 'house', at this 'meal', it is no kitchen table that we are
gathered round: this is the men's room. The lines are all
spoken by men, were all written by men. They tell of men's
deeds, men's meditations. Wait – here, at the very end,
while we are receiving our symbolic share in this massive
'love-feast', there is a hymn to Mary. I scan the words on
the sheet before me. Yes. It is as I thought. There is one
clear rôle only for women to follow: Mary is birther and
enabler and cherisher – for (her son) Christ's starring rôle.

My unease at the exclusively articulate men in Heaney's
'Station Island' is as nothing compared to my growing
hostility to the silence of and about women in this Mass.
There is, of course, no sign that any of the women here
objects in the slightest. We are all 'taking it like a woman'.
Even I, chameleon-pilgrim, sing the surface loveliness of the
words. I am wholly 'biddable and unforthcoming'. After all,
if I walk out of this performance, vote with my feet, there
is nowhere to go. I cannot walk on water like Christ, like
Peter. Coward, pragmatist, I cloak my rebellion: after all,
this is nothing to do with me any more, is it?

But I am here. I am touching the shoulders, the arms, of

those on each side of me. I have given and received the
two-handed gesture of peace. How can I judge what the
others' silence means, any more than they can judge mine?
I suddenly see that all of us, women and men, even the
starring clergy, are marginalised and diminished by the
same patriarchy. There is so much more kindness now, so
much more humanity than in the Church of my childhood.
It makes the unchanging wrongness, the lack of balance, all
the harder to bear. I cannot tell why my fellow pilgrims are
here, or why they are biddable: whether they still rejoice in
'the simple faith', or are here to make some reparation, or
to resolve some doubt. Some may be here, as in Kavanagh's
day, to strike some smug or some desperate bargain with
the deity. But a thousand individuals keep their counsel;
bow their heads as one for the final blessing: 'Go, the Mass
is ended.'

Where, for heaven's sake, does Heaney the pilgrim stand
on all this? Oh, not standing at all . . .

*   *   *

In *Stones of Aran*, Tim Robinson makes 'a circuit of [Aran's]
coast, whose features present themselves as stations of a
Pilgrimage'. Before he begins that (sunwise) circuit, he
remembers a moment years before when he stood thigh
deep in the sea off Aran watching 'two dolphins (or were
there three?) ... passing and repassing within a few yards
of [him]'. He ponders the problem of 'taking a single step
[that is] as adequate to the ground it clears as is the
dolphin's arc to its wave. Is it possible to think towards a
human conception of this "good step"? ... every step carries
us across geologies, biologies, myths, histories, politics,
etcetera, and trips us with the trailing *Rosa spinosissima* of
personal associations. To forget these dimensions of the
step is to forgo our honour as human beings, but an
awareness of them equal to the involuted complexities

under foot at any given moment would be a crushing
back-load to have to carry.'[1]

Heaney the pilgrim takes an 'adequate step', a step I am
frozen from taking. He sets foot in the other direction,
against the 'stream of pilgrims answering the bell': he is
'sunstruck', out in the unroofed outdoors. He doesn't even
stay for a bite and a sup.

He walks into childhood's playing at houses, but also
through centuries, through civilisations, through faiths. The
flock of today's faithful is hurdled away inside the basilica.
The ancient beds lie open to the sun, unpeopled. But out
here, on the cleared circles, the *genius* of the place
materialises for him, and she is unmistakably female –
girl-child, fairy, play-wife from 'mothers and fathers'.
'Freckle-face, fox-head, pod of the broom', she arrives as
mysteriously as the aisling of Ireland's eighteenth century
dream-vision poetry, but without the haunting distress that
hovers even over Ó Rathaille's loveliest 'Gile na gile' –
'Brightness of brightness I beheld on the way ...'[2] Heaney's
'she' brings affirmation, not distress: the rooted assurance
of a land that is not in subjection, and the promise of
fertility, of harvest. The 'tramped neolithic floor' of her
'house' is like a timeless threshing circle, ready for the gold
of the grain that will be spilled on it. The musk of an
unashamed sexuality is in the air: Innocence in the time
before Experience, bodies before the Fall.

Inside the built basilica there is only Mary, the virgin
mother, and Eve, mother of all our woe, to choose from.
Outside, there is the possibility of a sexual love innocent of
that polarity and all its works. This open air, this hallowed
and ancient place, is a setting now for sacraments that are
pagan and integral: here grain and wine will be both the
'outward signs of an inward grace', and still unmistakably
themselves; here even children playing at houses are
rehearsing a sacred and secret rite. No wonder Heaney's
pilgrim self 'shut[s his] ears to the bell', and walks away
into paganism and the timeless, mythic shelter of a tree.
The actual and fine-leaved solitary sycamore that has stood

by the largest of the beds for over three hundred years
offers, now, 'the bottle-green, still / shade of an oak': a
Roman oak, with perhaps a strain of the oaks that the
druids revered, and of the oakwood that gave Derry – *doire*
– its name. It may even have a slip of Eden in its
heartwood.

In this poem Heaney is at the halfway point in his
sequence, and at the threshold of adulthood in its
autobiographical sub-plot. It is rite of passage time. The
poem opens its heart to intimacy and to the female, moving
from the foxy eden of the freckle-faced girlchild to the
possibility of making 'grown-up' love. As the pilgrim
remembers his own passage to Experience, two long-dead
poets act as his invisible spiritual fosterers: Horace to urge
him to delight in the intelligence of the body's sensuality,
and another Italian, Dante, to give a mystical blessing to the
delight he finds.

They are *invisible* fosterers in the sense that neither is
named within the text. Each speaks an underword –
italicised to indicate its fragmentary, translated nature –
that is seamlessly integrated into Heaney's sonnet-stanzas.
He could, by being more showy about them, have had two
such charismatic poets act as creaking hinge points into
vast philosophical hinterlands, both pagan and Christian;
but this is a poem of hiddenness, not of big gestures: 'Eyes
shut. Leaf ears. *Don't tell. Don't tell.*' Any hinges are oiled
into silence in the text. In the sparse 'Notes' at the back of
the collection, their words are unobtrusively but precisely
attributed; follow the trail, and there, in the original context
of each quoted section, are some of the most radiant of the
silent women in (or, in this case, not in!) Heaney's whole
sequence. The effect is subtle and extraordinary. The light
it shines on this pivotal poem is, in the widest sense of the
word, religious.

'Shades of the Sabine farm / On the beds of Saint
Patrick's Purgatory.' Italy. Warm weather. Conviviality.
Imperial Rome's drop-out rural philosopher urges an easy
sensuality that is a far cry from Irish Catholicism in a cold

climate. What brings Horace to the narrow north? What can he offer Heaney except distress at such narrowness, and an unbearable contrast?

His very language sharpens the anomaly: Latin, the *lingua franca* shared, at different periods, by both the Imperial and the Holy Roman empires. For the bright schoolboy in Catholic Ireland, that long history would have been telescoped in a single day's hearing of the 'dead' tongue, the soft c's of the Mass's pronunciation and the hard c's of the schoolroom's making a fine, scholastic distinction. But Quintus Horatius Flaccus! What a dangerous thing even classroom learning can be – and what unsuitable rôle-models it can introduce to Catholic adolescents in the name of classical scholarship!

And was Horace also a presiding spirit at a later turning-point in Heaney's life? Both poets, having come from humble origins and achieved early literary acclaim, left the big city (Rome, Belfast) for rural seclusion, and devotion to their art. And they made the move – with the generous help of patrons – at a very similar age, their early thirties. The 'Glanmore Sonnets' are Heaney's celebratory 'odes' on that mid-life rural 'singing school' as much as they are his Ovidian 'Tristia' of (in his case chosen) exile. And the distinctive steep and wooded glens around Glanmore are an Irish approximation to the hill country beyond Tivoli where the house called Horace's can still be seen, its layout redeemed from vines and underbrush.[3]

For a still moment the carefree but serious Epicureanism of Horace's ode (the twenty-third of his third book) smiles on the stones of Station Island. Wine is the companion of philosophy, the loosener of anxiety and secrecy, the disabler of pomp and war. And when – best of all – Bacchus is accompanied by Venus, then living lanterns will light up the hours of darkness, '*Till Phoebus returning routs the morning star.*'

This, then, is the full context of the one line that Heaney carries over – 'trans-lates' – direct from the Latin. The reference is so swift and light of touch that only Heaney's clue would alert the reader to its discreet company. The goddess of love and her attendant Graces are its hidden women whose radiance leaves an afterglow even in this fragment of an ode. It is as though Horace's poem is a glass hologram: even a shard of it holds this image of Venus rejoicing.

And Heaney's poem unquestionably has woman in mind, even in this case when it leaves her out. A 'somnolent hymn to Mary' cuts across Horace's words in praise of sensuality – the Church's version of woman, exemplum of virginity and restraint. Despite 'leaf ears', and wine, and poetry, the twentieth century pilgrimage and its pieties are never quite out of the pilgrim's earshot. The resultant discord revives painful memories of 'long virgin / Fasts and thirsts' in a Catholic adolescence dominated by the intertwined guilts of ignorance and the confessional. The accoutrements of the land's fertility – 'bags of grain / And the sloped shafts of forks and hoes' – mock the boy's exclusion from such natural rhythms.

The abstinence and the guilt seem to last for years. Then, through a keyhole, through a window, a particular girl shines out both in her own perceived beauty and as an emblem of love's transforming kindness:

> ... that night I saw her honey-skinned
> Shoulder-blades and the wheatlands of her back
> Through the wide keyhole of her keyhole dress ...

She is wheat and honey, she is the boy's 'America, [his] new-found-land'. But the door is not yet opened, the window not shinned through; the girl has not revealed her face or her self. She keeps her back to the poem, and this reluctance of women to show their face within Heaney's text continues in the much fuller quotation from his second unseen fosterer – Dante.

For Heaney takes the lovely simile from near the end of the second canto of the *Inferno* and almost fills the sestet of his own concluding sonnet with his translation of it:

As little flowers that were all bowed and shut
By the night chills rise on their stems and open
As soon as they have felt the touch of sunlight,
So I revived in my own wilting powers
And my heart flushed, like somebody set free.

The lines are beautiful as they stand. But again a trail is quietly arrowed by the notes' precise attribution.

It is dusk on Good Friday, Dante's first day in Hell. His fear of 'the road and the pity' that lie before him[4] have disabled him utterly. Virgil has already rescued him from the wild beasts of worldly sin. Now it is his own infirmity of purpose, his own too-much thinking, that stop him in his tracks. But it is also now that he learns for the first time of the loving care of three women: Our Lady, Lucia and Beatrice are all watching over him from the court of heaven as he begins his arduous pilgrimage. And Beatrice, whom he loved on earth as Beatrice dei Portinari, is the very one who has sent Virgil to his side.

These 'tre donne gentile' enact with human grace and delicacy an allegorical model of divine grace: for the fearful Florentine it is grace abounding. It is this overflowing of love that revives him and frees him to continue both pilgrimage and poem. In Beatrice's words:

amor mi mosse, che mi fa parlare.
It is love that moves me, that makes me speak.[5]

The figures of the allegory – Mary the vessel of divine grace, Lucia its illumination, and Beatrice its wisdom – exist above and beyond the words that Heaney has translated, yet their presence in the canto from which he draws the simile leaves after-images that persist in its transplanted life, even more clearly than in the borrowing from Horace. Is it because, however remote the lost world of that great medieval architecture of faith, Dante's love of divine philosophy is rooted, like Heaney's own vision of love, in a very particular flesh-and-blood woman? In the *Commedia* human love becomes an expression of divine grace, and the individual beloved a bodying forth of Sophia, the wisdom of God.

What is Heaney doing here? It's possible that, far from objectifying and marginalising the female through his back-view-only icon of her presence, he may subtly be invoking Dante's help to express the elusive feminine within the psyche of us all, men as well as women. Both these male pilgrim-poets, Dante and Heaney, will have to learn about waiting, about not forcing either themselves, or others. 'This is the [feminine] way of non-interference and acceptance which has been praised by poets throughout the centuries,' writes Sukie Colegrave in *The Spirit of the Valley*, her investigation into the integration of the masculine and feminine within each of us. 'Trust is central to the feminine consciousness ... It is the capacity to surrender the individual ego to a meaning and direction which may not, at first, be intelligible.' Of the other side of the psyche, the masculine consciousness, she writes:

> It gives us the certainty that we stand utterly alone in this world, unsupported by institutions ... It brings the extraordinary and often alarming knowledge that we can look to no one and no thing other than ourselves for directions and answers.

She could have been writing about the demands that this very pilgrimage makes on its bewildered participants.

But why is it all quite so hidden in Heaney's poem? Am I too eager to discover such possibilities in his references simply because I am finding the Mass of my own pilgrimage so difficult, and Heaney's walking out of 'all that' so enviable? Surely he must have found something better out there in the open air of the deserted 'beds' than I have, held in the paternalistic embrace of the basilica! I hesitate, rethink that last Dantean lifting, its juxtaposition with the image of the girl's half-uncovered back. If he is indeed, by quoting Dante here, raising the possibility of a spiritual merging or consummation beyond the literal and physical, how is this to be achieved on any level within the remaining half of the sequence? For he is now moving into the most heavily masculine part of it, into other men's stories far more than his own. Just at the crucial point in his sub-plot of growing-up, just when an image of the feminine flickers almost into actuality on the island, he leaves the girl's image hanging, and it is faceless as well as voiceless.

There comes the uneasy feeling that Dante's image of the flowers rising up on their stems could suggest, in Heaney's rather different context, just a voyeur's arousal, and not a philosophical confirmation at all. Nor can I, at this moment, recall that there is any foreground narrative in the rest of the sequence that continues the story begun here into a face-to-face consummation. Will I find other, less literal, feminine presences to continue the 'argument' as I walk my new barefoot way through the difficult poems that I know are coming? Will it move on to a different plane altogether, and offer an indirect way forward from these radiant but disturbing images of the sixth poem?

NOTES

1. *Stones of Aran: Pilgrimage*, pp.11-13.
2. *An Duanaire*, edited by Seán Ó Tuama and Thomas Kinsella, No.49, pp.150-3.
3. See Gilbert Highet, *Poets in a Landscape*, pp.141ff.
4. *Inferno*, II, 4-5.
5. *Inferno*, II, 72.

CHAPTER NINE

I Was Dumb . . .

Poems VII & VIII

2 August 1987: early evening
  The Lough Derg Meal

... the contest on our side is not one of rivalry or vengeance, but of endurance. It is not those who can inflict the most, but those that can suffer the most who will conquer.

Terence MacSwiney,
Inaugural Speech as Mayor of Cork[1]

A penal cross found in the hand of a pilgrim
drowned in a boat accident during the 1795 pilgrimage season

Dry triangles of toasted white pan. Gritty circles of oatcake made to the island's uniquely glutinous recipe. How to choose which of these to break my fast with?

It is early evening: a long day travelled, and still I have swallowed nothing other than sips of water since last night, spent – where? Oh yes, at my cousin's house near Dublin, a place that is now utterly dim and remote in time as well as distance. The sensation of hunger, too, is strangely remote. It is common sense and curiosity, not the summoning of my stomach, that have brought me to the island's refectory to take the bare sustenance I will need to carry me through the night's vigil.

The kitchens are, of course, at the back of the women's hostel. No problem here about a rôle for female servers: check aprons are the vestments, great pots of black tea and coffee are the liquids poured into our proffered cups. We pilgrims sit on long benches at the simple wooden tables, and receive our daily bread. I dunk my toast in weak black instant coffee. It tastes surprisingly good.

Here, too, is a first chance to talk to fellow pilgrims about things other than the simple conduct of the pilgrimage, and to discover the inevitable connections that tie all the Irish together, whether by place or blood, by marriage or mutual friends. Sure enough, I find I am sitting with a nun and a teacher: only last week they were working together at Corrymeela[2] with an ex-Jesuit I knew very well at Oxford (when he was still a Jesuit). I haven't seen him for over twelve years, but his name – and style – are unmistakable in their telling.

Immediately, Sister Thérèse, Nuala and I are intimates. They introduce their companion to me: Billy, a clerical student from a 'good' Dublin family who has never dreamed of 'doing Lough Derg', but has been talked into it by them at the last minute while staying up North. With a name like Billy, I wonder that the Northern Catholics have had any dealings with him![3] Each of the women has her own, more considered reason for being here. Thérèse works with alcoholics, and recently pledged (to God, not the

court) that she would do The Station if one of her clients
were let off a jail sentence. He was – so here she is. Nuala
has come for a reason that interests me more: after years of
being lapsed she has just rediscovered her faith – through
Our Lady of Medjugorje.

A few weeks ago she went to Yugoslavia – she's still not
sure how she ever got into the trip – to visit the site
acclaimed by Europe's Catholics as the latest place to be
blessed with apparitions of Mary. There was Lourdes, then
Fatima, and now Medjugorje: in each place, Mary has
appeared to children or teenagers with urgent messages of
repentance for the whole world. Despite what she thought
was healthy scepticism, Nuala was deeply moved by the
charisma of the young villagers who were even then still
receiving the apparitions, and 'all this [she] w[as] clear of
[she] walked into / over again' – and with joy. She is here
on the island in unreserved thanksgiving.

So much of the talk is of Mary's apparitions! Just
recently, she has been appearing in Ireland, too. Down in
Co. Cork, her statue at the grotto in Ballinspittle has been
clearly seen to move – crowds of the faithful have
witnessed it night after night. And it's not just in Cork.
Over in Sligo, Mary has been appearing in a field by the
river for several evenings recently, and regular prayers are
being said by the growing crowds. I am told how a couple
of farmers were wiring up a hasty public address system
powered by a car battery they had housed in an old biscuit
tin, when – didn't Mary come and glimmer on the very
pole itself over their heads? And wasn't the despairing joke
of the losing side during the last All Ireland hurling final,
'Sure, if only our men were statues of the Virgin, they'd be
getting more of a move on'?

I am struck by Mary's extraordinary persistence. Despite
being carefully hedged about by theological limitations, she
seems to have an autonomy in these apparitions that is well
calculated to upset hierarchies: in Yugoslavia she is causing
dissension among both the bishops *and* the communist
administrators of the region. In Ireland the 'authorities' sit

uncomfortably on the drystone wall. She takes shape and voice in the yearnings of ordinary people. Does she answer, in these unofficial and unsettling apparitions, a hunger in them that is unanswered in the everyday practice of their religion? At Medjugorje and Ballinspittle, she has not yet – though it's happening fast – been entirely taken over by institutions, or the materialist and sugary crystallisations of piety.

I realise that I must think again about the ideal and myth of Mary, and must hold over against the Church's bland and passive virgin-mother a new image: stirrer of the status quo, woman acting on her own, even outlaw. A despairing conclusion of Marina Warner's book, *Alone Of All Her Sex*, that the myth of Mary 'endorses the most pessimistic and world-denying self-sacrifice as the state of the elect'[4] suddenly seems in need of qualification. There is a sense in which an autonomous Mary, with an urgent message of peace and non-materialism, is here and now taking on an active rôle outside official structures. Superstition and mass-hysteria, much resorted to by the hostile, seem inadequate and simplistic as explanations. Is there a rising up of a renewed and renewing feminine consciousness amongst the most passive of the faithful? I remember from somewhere the bold thesis of the American theologian, Elizabeth Gould Davis, that 'the only reality in Christianity is Mary, the Female Principle, the ancient goddess reborn'.[5]

(Later, back home with my books, I will track down her words, and also this:

> Davis claims that it was the discovery, attributed to St Patrick, that the pagans would accept Christ only if they could have Mary that changed the official policy toward Mary in the church.[6]

Was it in the stone and water fastness of Lough Derg, where he spent so long and lonely a retreat, that Patrick made his peace and pact with the goddess?)

'Best not to eat too much.' The experienced Sister Thérèse touches Billy's sleeve as he reaches out for yet another slice of toast. 'You'll only feel the pangs more on the morrow.' I follow her advice too, and we leave the refectory together: all four of us were late arrivals, and still have two complete stations to do before the night vigil.

It feels like the first day at a new school when at last you have found a gang. Now I look out for them, and smile, as we do our rounds. 'Let's stick together during the vigil,' says Nuala. 'Oh yes, let's.' I feel I am back in the crowd of belonging.

As I walk the long and the short circles of my second station, I think further about the contradictory messages of the figure of Mary; of the tragic split in Christianity's understanding of the feminine. I remember my unease at the Mass earlier, my feeling that all of us, men as well as women, were involved in an unavoidable diminishment. What binds me still to this congregation after years well out of it? Is it the strange sense that we are all, in some derogatory – and peculiarly Christian – sense, 'women'? This religion of my childhood, the religion, moreover, of the West for two millennia, seems to require of all its followers the docility and self-abnegation that its ideal female – its Mary –. bodies forth.

Even Christ, I realise with a small shock as two disparate areas of my thinking knock against each other, takes on at times this circumscribed, fractured womanhood. The chief icon in the 'kitchen grottoes' of Ireland's Catholic homes is still the delicately featured 'Sacred Heart', a meek and mild Jesus whose beard is merely a silken trimming at the edge of a very feminine chin. Below, his most uncarpenter-like hand points to the raw bared heart in his chest. There is little to distinguish him from Our Lady of the Sorrows, another popular icon of suffering that displays an open-heart chest beneath a pale and feminine face – a heart pierced this time by the seven swords of Mary's worst griefs. These rôle-models of love are unrelievedly passive and bloody – what victims they seem! Yes, they reply, and *you* are one of my tormentors when you sin.

As we circle the basilica at the beginning of our third station, Sister Thérèse happens to be alongside me, and suggests that she say the decades of the rosary with me. 'Yes,' I say, but that is all I can say, for when she finishes the first part of the first Hail Mary I find I cannot utter the response. It seems impossible that I have forgotten words said so many times in my life, and already hundreds of times this day; but I cannot now say them aloud – in fact, I cannot retrieve them at all in my mind.

'And blessed is the fruit of thy womb, Jesus,' she tries again, ending this time with the rising tone of a question. I cannot even fumble a consent in rigmarole to this central prayer of Mariolatry, and must plead tiredness because I cannot plead apostasy, not just now, and not to Thérèse. She nods and moves on, giving me a puzzled look.

The amnesia is not consciously chosen but, after the panic and embarrassment subside, I am half-pleased by it. I want to hold on to the glimpse I had of an autonomous Mary, a woman not defined by motherhood or 'God' at all. I quickly devise an alternative system of recitation that will carry me through the endless prayers before me: a slow and rhythmic count to ten should cover each Hail Mary; twelve, say, for an Our Father; and about seventeen will do for the Apostles' Creed. With a little stretching and trimming this proves about right, even when I am once more going round the stone beds. What a relief! I now have a workable scheme for word-survival, a set of mantras I can inhabit without any trace of meaning.

Daylight leaches away slowly when one is intent and out of doors. The wind is chill now even in the sheltered parts, and the island clergy (distinguishable from the many priests who are on pilgrimage with us by their glossy black shoes) begin to hover near the beds, like the shepherds they are named for, and chivvy the last late treaders of the stones. It is time for Night Prayer, and the commencement of our vigil. Once more we answer the bell, and crowd into the basilica. But the crush is only for a short time. Night Prayer

is quickly said, and then our numbers are halved. Those
who kept vigil the previous night are sent at last to their
one night of rest. The great candle of their vigil is
extinguished, and a new, ominously taller, one is lit – for
ours.

The doors of the basilica are ceremonially bolted. We are
locked in for our first indoor station of this longest night,
an immuring that is the only symbolic survival of the
medieval pilgrim's experience of being walled into
Purgatory's cave. I am entering deeper and deeper into the
pilgrimage's movements, but I am less and less involved in
its words.

                    *   *   *

Fresh and refreshed from inhaling 'the land of kindness',
the pilgrim Heaney stays firmly outside any walls. He is
down by the water's edge, in a chosen and sustained
solitude that is highly irregular in Lough Derg's communal
worship. Under the oak tree of Poem VI he has been
confirmed – strengthened, that is; not at all 'confirmed' in
the Church's narrow sense. '[A] window facing the deep
south of luck / Opened ...' Luck, not grace, after all.

It is the last image of delight for a long time. Even at a
simple human level this absconding pilgrim needs any kind
of confirmation he can get, any shred of golden light, as he
begins to face the second half of his dream-journey: the
darkening 'road and the pity' that lead so soon now into
the realm of his and his community's untimely and
violently dead.

Looking at the water 'as if it were a clear barometer / or
a mirror', he is in an anteroom to adulthood: the ghost he
is about to meet will reminisce about their courting days;
they had played football, too, as young men. But it is also
an anteroom to violence and to sacrifice, and to particular
tragedies in Ulster's current conflict. Does he see his own
face reflected in that water before he fails to see his
friend's?

>   [H]is reflection
>   did not appear but I sensed a presence
>   entering into my concentration
>
>   on not being concentrated as he spoke
>   my name.

Like the other ghosts, this man offers a version of 'the path
not taken' by their living visitant. And comes closer –
through friendship, peer-group – to Heaney's own
condition than did the ghosts behind the basilica.

Heaney's urge 'to bow down, to offer up', voiced at the
end of his earlier poem 'At the Water's Edge', infuriated me
in January by Lough Erne, made me feel that what he was
responding to was everything that is unnacceptable to me
as a woman in Catholicism. Now he is at the very water's
edge that he longed for then; he has 'gone foetal' and will
'go penitential'. I remain suspicious, wary. But in this
narrative of almost somnambulist acceptance of violent
death, I come to realise how complex and entrapping
self-sacrifice can be for men also.

Passivity, I have realised, is by no means reserved to
women in Christianity's divided consciousness. It is as if
the whole problem of authority has been defined by
polarising all of us within stereotyped gender definitions,
and making the faithful – and Christ himself in certain
situations – take upon themselves a caricature of the
feminine: emotionalism, passivity, self-abnegation, and most
of all (though *not* at all, of course, in Christ's case!) sin.
Those in positions of authority, from God the Father and
his son (in more robust rôle) down to his earthly
spokesmen, take on an equally limiting caricature of the
masculine: 'objective' and super-rational certainty, the
willingness to dominate and manipulate others 'for the
higher good', and the aggression needed to pursue their
vision of justice.

I had a glimpse of the un-polarising and reconciling of
these unhelpful extremes of feminine and masculine in the

radiant ending of Poem VI. As Heaney turns from that brief and ambiguous moment of unrealised possibility into a world that is almost exclusively male, the subtext of the feminine and its problematical place in the lives of Catholic men (and all men?) becomes more insistent. To be a Catholic in the Protestant state of Northern Ireland is to be reared in a lower caste, to be oppressed from birth, to be excluded from the centres of power and money: a caste that women the world over are born into. And, as is so for women, there are two broad strategies of coping: the 'feminine' ways of acceptance, connivance, the guilt of self-blame; or the 'masculine' ways of analysis, displacement – or violence.

In this first meeting (in the sequence) with a soul caught up in Ulster's war, both poet *and* ghost are eerily passive. The ghost, victim of a notorious sectarian killing, tells his own story of the night he died, and with deceptive and colloquial ease. The solid normality of the man weights it down to circumstance and place – a small town grocery, an 'old landrover', killers who are known to him and do not wear disguise.

In the telling, however, the shopkeeper takes on elements of Christ's peculiarly submissive rôle as willing sacrificial victim. When Heaney himself refers to his friend as 'the perfect, clean, unthinkable victim' he echoes unmistakably the prayer *Unde et memores* that is said just after the consecration of the bread and wine in the Mass: it offers Christ to the Father as '*hostiam puram, hostiam sanctam, hostiam immaculatam* – 'a pure, a holy, a spotless victim'.

The man's own account is extraordinary for its calm air of inevitability, ruffled only by a brief impatience with his wife's weeping and her panicky queries – which were utterly justified, of course, in the event. At the time, it is as though they are distractions that threaten to deflect him from a path he must take, alone, to a ritual death. 'Is your head / astray, or what's come over you?' he 'roar[s]' at her, much as Christ roared 'Get thee behind me, Satan!' at Peter when he begged Christ to evade the death he had foreseen. And the man's recognition of the faces of his intending murderers in the light of the street lamp has shades of the Judas story in it: he is betrayed into violent death by those who are personally known to him, and he accepts this with no demur.

The Christ whose image lies behind the shaping of this story is the Lamb of God, Jesus meek and mild: the Christ who follows the (partial) feminine path of submission to the Father. The dead shopkeeper does not display a red heart in an opened chest like the holy pictures of the Sacred Heart, but he does offer an icon of 'ravaged forehead and blood' that recalls the thorn-ravaged, suffering face of Christ in depictions of the Passion.

The reaction of the pilgrim Heaney to this sectarian murder, this 'particularly notorious incident in Co. Antrim'[7] for which two off-duty policemen were later found guilty, is unexpected, even to himself:

> 'Forgive the way I have lived indifferent –
> forgive my timid circumspect involvement,'
>
> I surprised myself by saying.

Anger in some form is to be expected, surely, but this is anger directed inwards to become that most familiar of Catholic emotions, guilt. The ghost of the murdered man dismisses the plea with incomprehension: '"Forgive / my eye," he said, "all that's above my head."' His unquestioning acceptance of so violent an end is disquieting. It's as if his dying was 'just part of the job'. Heaney's attempt to widen the discussion embarrasses him as much as his wife's 'nagging' and lamenting did at the time.

*   *   *

When the figure of the murdered shopkeeper has 'trembled like a heatwave and faded', the pilgrim finds himself up the slope and away from the water's edge, though the black and white of its furrowed surface are still in his eye. At the beginning of Poem VIII he is on his knees, and 'at the hard mouth of St Brigid's Bed'. But no, he isn't beginning to 'do his station' properly at last, as a change from all that walking the wrong way, and walking out. For it seems that this bending of the knee is merely part of a dream within a dream: the black and white of the waters soon take shape as a bird of ill omen, a single magpie for bad luck that 'staggers' into his field of vision, and

> I came to and there at the bed's stone hub
> was my archaeologist, very like himself, ...

After this 'coming to' there is no further mention of kneeling or of conventional prayer to a saint or deity. Instead, Heaney the pilgrim seems to be suing for understanding and forgiveness from a friend and fellow human. The archaeologist's death is – though cruelly premature – natural in the sense that he is not the victim of violence. And the two men had, and here have again, time and place to make their farewells. Yet the distinctive involvement of each of them with Ulster's long history casts shadows of self-doubt over this last meeting, and ghost and pilgrim go over and over their memories of it, haunted by the failure in communication. Their conversation on Purgatory's island tries to be a sort of two-handed, secular 'sacrament of reconciliation' (the new name, I discover on the island, for 'Confession'), tries to get it right *this time*. But neither man quite manages it. Each is so taken up with his own guilts that he cannot reach out and touch the other's pain.

Heaney, reduced to banter 'too early in that [hospital] visit', is troubled afresh by his own decision in 1972 to leave the North and become a full-time poet in the comparative haven of the South. For the unhealed bedside

farewell that still haunts him on Station Island took place
after that chosen exile began:

> I had to head back straight away to Dublin,
> guilty and empty, feeling I had said nothing
> and that, as usual, I had somehow broken
> covenants, and failed an obligation.

Covenants have been broken, the very formality and
inclusiveness suggests, not just with his friend but with the
North itself. How far should the 'vocation' of poetry be
allowed to overrule the very pieties that nourished it into
being? This is a question that ran through *North* and
Fieldwork. Here on Saint Brigid's bed the poet faces it within
a memory of such pain that he could not in that hospital
ward – and still cannot – find words to voice it. Yet words
are the very medium of his craft.

Although Tom Delaney's ghost[8] seems uninterested in
the artistic dilemma of his friend, he responds with his own
version of a calling so closely followed that he has lost
touch with aspects of its meaning, and aspects of his ability
to communicate with others. He talks of being 'half-
numbed' with his beloved and 'familiar stone', and so taken
up with the detail of his 'still-faced archaeology' that he has
dug

> for years in that hard place
in a muck of bigotry under the walls
picking through shards and Williamite cannon balls[.]
But all that we just turned to banter too.

The masculine ability to compartmentalise aspects of a life,
to divorce and displace intellectual excitement from whole
areas of the self and society, has left him with fragments
rather than a consoling vision.[9]

It seems that, despite all their expertise in words and
history, both men sense that their individual utterances
have become hollow and involuted; and now, with the

approaching death of one of them, their conversing too is
reduced to silence. Even their attempts at visual or physical
contact fail.

> 'Did our long gaze and last handshake contain
> nothing to appease that recognition?'
> 'Nothing at all. ...'

Both as professionals and as friends, this is an appalling
failure in communication to have to admit to, although
their very anguish at this breakdown is a testament to the
importance of their friendship to each of them.

And in Heaney's physical description of his friend there
is a another bittersweet link between them: they are
'woodkernes' both. In the poem that most eloquently and
ambivalently expresses the *angst* of his Glanmore exile –
'Exposure' in   *Fieldwork* – Heaney called himself 'a
wood-kerne / Escaped from the massacre'. On Station
Island he first recognises his friend's ghost by 'the wing /
of woodkerne's hair [that] fanned down over his brow'. It's
a term, dating from the time of Elizabeth I's conquest of
Ireland, for the ill-equipped native soldiery who were able
to melt in and out of the forests. 'Outlaws', the O.E.D. has
it. Sixteenth century guerrillas . . . ? But neither man has
taken the obvious and literal twentieth century woodkerne
rôle – the archetypally 'masculine' rôle – of armed
resistance to the occupying force. Their calling was –
surely? – to 'serve their country' in more subtle and
spiritual ways.

But their mood in this remembered meeting suggests
that poetry and/or archaeology became for both of them
unwitting displacement activities, a funnelling of energy
into 'work'. Their skilled and specialised ways of looking
grew self-reflexive, self-validating; and are finally revealed,
in the uncompromising naked light of the deathbed, to be
out of true. And for Heaney in particular, the danger of
'digging' turning into 'digging in' comes too close to the
bone.

In *North*, of course, written mainly in the immediate aftermath of moving South, Heaney was both poet *and* archaeologist. It was a time of great general excitement in the South about 'Viking Dublin',[10] but Heaney's poems homed in on one nexus of themes – those finds (not just in Ireland) suggestive of a passive and sacrificial past that he saw as 'emblematic' of the present position in the North. The extraordinary passivity of all the actors (including the poet) in Part I of *North* made Edna Longley call it 'a book of martyrs rather than tragic protagonists.'[11] (Even the Vikings themselves, arriving 'suddenly ... in violence and epiphany', offer the poet, once they *have* arrived, only the uncharacteristically quietist advice: 'Lie down / in the word-hoard ...'.[12])

It was at this period, I remember, that Heaney was writing about 'the Goddess' in prose as well as poetry: Ireland's 'indigenous territorial numen, a tutelar of the whole island ...' and her links with, among others, Jutland's 'Mother Goddess, the goddess of the ground who needed new bridegrooms each winter to bed with her in her sacred place, in the bog ...'.[13]

There is little in this bleak part of the 'Station Island' sequence of the unrelenting circularity of *North*, its 'these things have always happened; they happened then, they happen now'[14] romantic fatalism. 'Station Island' may be less seductive than the Bog poems in its language, but it is also less manhandled, less deliberately architectonic in structure.[15] It is more a dream than a drilling operation – Heaney used the image of an auger to describe the downward-digging short-lined stanzas of *North*'s archaeological poems. The ghosts of purgatory rise up, apparently unbidden, like the face in the very first and most compelling of the Bog poems, 'Tollund Man'. Though 'they dug him out', he seems to surface actively in Heaney's vision of him, as poems themselves do according to the early account of inspiration in *Preoccupations*, rather than wait in passivity to be discovered by invasive instruments.[16]

There is no comfortable conclusion to the meeting with
the archaeologist:
> '... dead at thirty-two!
> Ah poet, lucky poet, tell me why
> what seemed deserved and promised passed me by?'

Then two ambivalent images, of crafted finds from periods
before and after the Vikings', float before the pilgrim as he
stands, speechless once more, at the bed named for Saint
Brigid. First he sees a vision from a museum-case in the
Ulster Museum: the Malone Hoard (found in the university
quarter of Belfast), a collection of basalt axe heads that are
plump and shiny as black eggs. Are they symbols of
aggression, or of new life? There isn't time to find out, for
next a still and 'mild-mouthed' woman's face comes into
view,
> a face
> he had once given me, a plaster cast
> of an abbess, done by the Gowran master, ...

This, I think wryly, is a statue that does not move. And
isn't it – though undoubtedly 'a character of grace' – just
one more emblem of passivity and the unusable past?
Sure enough, when the next ghost forces his bleeding
and mud-plastered body into the pilgrim's sight, he taunts
the poet with having been at one of Ireland's finest old
abbeys when news of *his* death in the North came through:
Jerpoint in Co. Kilkenny, 'a most picturesque ruin'.[17]
There's no place in this dead man's reckoning for the old
pieties of that long-gone period of faith, or for the
courtesies of art.

> You were there with poets when you got the word
> and stayed there with them, while your own flesh and
>   blood
> was carted to Bellaghy from the Fews.

With this rude arrival of Heaney's second cousin comes the

most thorough and considered attack yet on his own poetic
vocation, and his humanity: the subject of one of his finest
elegies repudiates, with all the vituperative skill the poet
can give him, the words, the intentions, the very man
himself who could write 'The Strand at Lough Beg',[18] and
offer a poem's 'fitting emblems of adversity', with its
erudite echoes of Dante, rather than his simple human
presence as a mourner.

> You confused evasion and artistic tact.
> The Protestant who shot me through the head
> I accuse directly, but indirectly, you
> who now atone perhaps upon this bed
> for the way you whitewashed ugliness and drew
> the lovely blinds of the *Purgatorio*
> and saccharined my death with morning dew.

Since coming to the edge of the water, Heaney the pilgrim
has been confined to indoor visions: the grocer's shop in
County Antrim, the hi-tech hospital ward in the city. The
world of moist and vegetable growth that sustains his
spirits elsewhere has been far from him. Now his cousin
Colum McCartney angrily denies him even the consolation
of the strand at Lough Beg that he had turned to in his first
shock of grief. He tries in vain to explain his first shocked
reaction to the news:

> I kept seeing a grey stretch of Lough Beg
> and the strand empty at daybreak.
> I felt like the bottom of a dried-up lake.

Imagining it and speaking it forth in words had flooded the
drought of that moment with the world of wet, Heaney's
and McCartney's heartland, all 'squeaking sedge', drizzle
and 'rushes that shoot green again'. But imagination runs
hard up against 'fact'. His cousin's answer will brook no
such plea:

You saw that, and you wrote that – not the fact.

Poetry, the past, the mild-mouthed face of woman, nature's world of growing and decay, wise passiveness, sacrifice – all this ragbaggy nexus of ideas seems to be rubbished here, on the station's smallest, tightest circle, its sharpest stones. All that Heaney perceives as feminine in his craft and in his life, in his people and in his landscape, seems powerless and despised. How is he to reconcile that creative capacity for surrender and 'listening out' with the feminine's shadow side of passivity and sacrifice? And where is he to look for a masculine principle that does not in the end cut him off from his community and his deepest self?

His response when put on the spot by Colum MacCartney is still trapped hopelessly within the passive mode:

I was dumb, encountering what was destined.

NOTES

1.   Terence MacSwiney died in Brixton Prison, after a seventy-four-day hunger strike, on 25 October 1920. A playwright and a leading nationalist, he was still Lord Mayor of Cork at the time of his death. His suffering and end received widespread sympathetic attention round the world, especially amongst other nascent nationalist and anti-colonialist movements. He is commemorated annually on this side of the water by the London-based Terence MacSwiney Lecture series.

2.   The Corrymeela Centre is an interdenominational centre on the north Antrim coast devoted to promoting reconciliation between the communities in the North of Ireland.

3.   William of Orange made even the naming of flowers problematic for Catholics in the North when I was a child: sweet-william was commonly known as 'stinking Billy'.

4.   Marina Warner, *Alone of All Her Sex*, p.337.

5.   *The First Sex*, p.246, quoted in *Beyond God the Father* by Mary Daly, p.92.

6.   Ibid.

7.   Neil Corcoran, *Seamus Heaney*, p.162.

8.   The archaeologist's name: see ibid.

9.   Compare 'An Afterwards' in *Fieldwork*, where the poet's wife upbraids him for his exclusive involvement in poetry. The lending of a voice of detailed and hard-hitting criticism to another in this poem is a forerunner of the increasingly harsh arraignments of the 'Station Island' sequence.

10.   The excitement culminated, sadly, in an unsuccessful attempt to prevent Dublin City Council from bulldozing one of the most extensive and well-preserved Viking sites yet found in Northern Europe (Wood Quay) and building new council offices on it.

11.   *Poetry in the Wars*, p.155.

12.   In the title poem 'North'.

13.   *Preoccupations*, p.57.

14.   Ciaran Carson in *The Honest Ulsterman* No.50, p.184.

15.   Edna Longley suggests that in Part I of *North* we see 'a conflict in Heaney (amply evidenced by *Preoccupations*) between an instinctive, 'feminine' artesian procedure ... and an ordering, 'male' architectonic procedure ... Stylistic examination suggests that Heaney has upset his strategic brinkmanship, his former complex creative balance, by applying architectonic methods to artesian matters, by processing his rich organic resources into hard-edged blocks.' Op. cit., pp.163/4.

16.   'Tollund Man' was published on its own in *Wintering Out*, the collection before *North*. Compare 'I have always listened for poems, they come sometimes like bodies come out of a bog, almost complete, seeming to have been laid down a long time ago, surfacing with a touch of mystery.' *Preoccupations*, p.34.

17.   *The AA Book of Ireland*, 1950, p.250.

18.   In *Fieldwork*.

CHAPTER TEN

The Hour of Lead

Poem IX

2–3 August 1987: The night vigil
January 1987: Belfast in the snow

Other forms were near. His soul had approached that
region where dwell the vast hosts of the dead. He was
conscious of, but could not apprehend, their wayward
and flickering existence. His own identity was fading
out into a grey impalpable world: the solid world
itself, which these dead had one time reared and lived
in, was dissolving and dwindling.

James Joyce, 'The Dead'

Lough Neagh strand, near Toome

In the locked basilica we do a station of the mind. One pilgrim from amongst us stands at a lectern and leads us in the prayers. It is like a mass play-reading in which we chant our chorus-part in dull unison while we are 'walked through' our moves. Our cantor reads the stage directions in 'Order of Station' imperatives: 'Walk slowly, by your right hand ... Kneel at the entrance to the Bed ... Walk six times around the outside of the large Penitential Bed ... Go to the water's edge; stand, and say ...' We pace in spirit the ground that earlier we have walked for real, in the open – and as comparative individuals.

We kneel, we stand, we walk, according to our imagined place in the exercises. Barefoot still, we shuffle the walked parts in a great impromptu procession that swings out and round the aisles of the basilica. Some of us choose to tighten our circuits by cutting from aisle to aisle between two pews; a few pace continually up and down the same pew in a private and straight furrow. But wherever we walk, however angular our 'circle', we always turn to our right, sunwise, although the sun has long since set behind the hills outside. And we kneel, we stand, wherever the order of the station decrees it, usually on the cold and marble floor: it is a weary way down and then up again.

The sound of the responses swells with the same cadences over and over again, the same indistinguishable syllables leading up to each prayer's emphatic 'a-*men*'. There are no gaps in the rhythm. Leader and congregation always cut in a second or two before the other has finished. It is a dream game of musical statues in which the main drone never ceases. We drop and rise at the command of the cantor. We are circle-bashing, an exhausted army on a long march to nowhere.

It is after one in the morning. It is after three. Each station takes nearly an hour to wind its way round and round the great interior. There are four of them to get through before Mass at 6.30 a.m. Between stations we are sent out into the night air and blowing rain for half an hour or so to recover, or to the smoke-filled Night Shelter that

rides out over the lake waters on piles like a rickety old
ferryboat in dry dock. People pass the time there in
touchingly ordinary ways: playing card-games, knitting,
flicking through magazines – and of course, 'the crack'. Too
soon the pitiless bell summons us back, and, as the Hail
Marys begin once more, it is as if we had never left this
swaying, pale interior.

People are beginning to nod off now during the kneeling
prayers. Over there a mountainy man with a sharp face is
keeping a look-out, and goes across to jab any such weak
vessels awake. They even thank him! At one point I see
that Billy, the clerical student, caught up in a slow-moving
shuffle, is actually asleep on his feet. He only stumbles into
waking when the press of pilgrims round him eases, and
no longer holds him vertical.

'The worst'll be the fourth station of the night,' Thérèse,
the old hand, has warned us. 'Say about five in the
morning. And the Mass, then, is hard to get through, very
hard. I'd be sorry for the priest who'd worked hard on his
sermon. Sure at least half of us won't be conscious for it!'

Hunger is nowhere in this vigil; even boredom is
strangely suspended. It is sleep that drags at us and
threatens to pull us down. Staying awake demands a level
of concentration that I last remember needing when I was
in labour. The pressure for sleep comes in waves that arrive
closer and closer together, like the unmanageable pain of
contractions that I must again and again rise to, find ways
of getting over and through.

There are hundreds of us halting a common way,
apparently moving together. But each of us is becoming
more and more alone. We are solitaries, women and men
of the road who persist strangely in muttering our way
through a thousand private purgatories . . . lost, fumbling
singly through snow . . . desperately fighting the soft, the
marshmallow world of sleep.

> This is the Hour of Lead –
> Remembered, if outlived,

As Freezing persons, recollect the Snow –
First – Chill – then Stupor – then the letting go –[1]

* * *

January. Belfast. Everything white under snow. In all my imagined returns to the city of my childhood, there was never *snow*! Such an uncommon weather in that damp sea-city, where one season trickled rainily into the next. Or so I remember it. And did the hills always hang this close over the west of the city – or is it that their out-of-the-ordinary whiteness leans on perspective?

I take the car off the unknown of the M2 and Westlink road system, and turn south from the city centre. From under the snow, despite demolition and reconstruction, despite the sunset-strip sign language of the eighties, the familiar outlines and layouts shine through. The Donegall Road. Shaftesbury Square. I even see Greaves the grocer's on the corner of Bradbury Place where the monochrome of snow tidies the bulldozed ground of a building site. It still has an existence in my mind's unexpected and detailed archive. I find that I am rebuilding 'my' part of Belfast as I move through the Belfast of twenty years later. Unerringly I find my way home.

But I am not yet ready to look at the house I grew up in. I accelerate past its road-end. 'I'm going to take you to the Giant's Ring while it's still light,' I tell Michael. Suddenly it's important to set foot there before anywhere, on that megalithic site at the city's boundary, a mile or less from my house. Across the Lagan, then. Hills have been levelled, valleys made smooth on the road that used to go steeply down to the river. There's a new bridge, but the Minnowburn Beeches are still a dense wood on the river's south bank, and the narrow lane still climbs up to the right through their thinning cover, and out on to bare pasture.

A small car-park. An 'ancient monument' sign. There is

no one else about. The dolmen stands, shrunk but intact, in
the midst of its huge enclosure. Above its white ramparts
the frost-thickened air is red with the afterlight of sunset.
'This is one of the wonderful things about Belfast,' I say to
Michael. 'The wild hills and the ancient holy places are
right in, close to the city.' 'And cared for, too,' he replies.
We dance about together to get warm, both delighted, for
our different reasons, that I did not make this first return to
the city of my childhood without him.

But when we arrive, chilly but radiant, at the house of
the old friend who is putting us up, her response to where
we have just come from is a shudder. 'Oh – I never go
there any more. No, not for years. Not since a really nasty
sectarian murder was done there – or at least, the body – it
was mutilated – they dumped it right in the Ring.' We do
not ask from which 'side' the victim came, which 'side' the
assassin.

I wonder what gut-feeling took me up there, and let me
be so blithe. How ignorant I am of this once-loved city! Oh,
I didn't want to leave it. I grieved and raged at seventeen
when our house was stripped down to its pieced
floorboards, and our belongings were auctioned or crated
up for shipment 'across the water'. But afterwards how
remote I allowed it to become – until dreams and
nightmares began their insidious summonings back.

Outside the snow starts falling thickly again. I take
Michael to a window at the front of my friend's house, and
point across the muffled gardens opposite. The house I
grew up in is just two suburban roads away. Tomorrow,
perhaps, I will take him there. But I do not say that another
house is in my mind's eye: my uncle's, in the road between.
Beyond the slope and the long gardens, hidden in snow's
yellow light, is the house where he opened his door one
weekday morning to violent death: to a teenage IRA
gunman who had hijacked a GPO van and its driver's
uniform and bag. The first the neighbours knew of it in that
quiet road was the oddness of a post-van speeding away
up the hill – like a get-away car, they said. My uncle's

eight-year-old daughter stood at the back of their hallway behind his fallen body: she had seen it all.[2]

Untimely death and loss are wounds that the survivors never quite recover from. We live on, the walking wounded, stiff with scar tissue, learning anew and anew how to keep moving, adapting; we forget for a little, then stumble again into unmanageable grief, even after years have passed. The dead themselves seem to alter, as we alter in their absence. But in Ireland those who have died by violence grow and change in relation to all the living, not just to the individuals who loved – or hated – them in life. Some, like my uncle, haunt us with their now never-to-be-spoken contributions to the search for peace. Some walk alongside their survivors with an odour of martyrdom – if not always of sanctity – about them: 'The man that dies has the chief part in the story.'[3] So many undone by death, and who refuse to die . . . Suddenly, Heaney's Station Island seems far too underpopulated for an Ulster underworld I imagine the island as crowded as the banks of the Styx, with a throng of souls 'multitudinous as the leaves that fall in a forest / at the first frost of autumn.'[4]

'It had begun to snow again ...' I cannot keep that last scene of 'The Dead' out of my mind.

Yes, the newspapers were right: snow was general all over Ireland. It was falling on every part of the dark central plain, on the treeless hills, falling softly upon the Bog of Allen and, farther westward, softly falling into the dark mutinous Shannon waves. It was falling, too, upon every part of the lonely churchyard on the hill where Michael Furey lay buried. It lay thickly drifted on the crooked crosses and headstones, on the spears of the little gate, on the barren thorns. His soul swooned slowly as he heard the snow falling faintly through the universe and faintly falling, like the descent of their last end, upon all the living and the dead.[5]

Forty miles to the north-west, and west of the Bann River
(the North's equivalent to Joyce's Shannon), very close to
the road that my Michael and I have driven that afternoon,
snow is falling on the burial grounds of Saint Mary's
Church, Bellaghy: on the grave of Colm Gerard McCartney
in the old enclosure, 'A martyr for his faith'; and, in the
new burial ground over the road, on the double grave of
two other local men who also died in their twenties: Francis
Hughes and Thomas McElwee, the second and the second-
last of the ten men to die during the 1981 hunger strike.
And there will surely be fresh flowers laid there under the
snow.

                    *   *   *

OLDEST PUPIL   *When did he sicken?*
                Is it a fever that is wasting him?
KING   *No fever or sickness. He has chosen death:*
                Refusing to eat or drink, that he may bring
                Disgrace upon me; for there is a custom,
                An old and foolish custom, that if a man
                Be wronged, or think that he is wronged, and
                                                    starve
                Upon another's threshold till he die,
                The common people, for all the time to come,
                will raise a heavy cry against that threshold,
                Even though it be the King's.[6]

*... great emphasis was placed by the authorities on the
'criminality' of terrorism ... And, of course, special category
status was abolished, to remove the formal distinctions
between paramilitary prisoners and 'common' criminals ...*[7]

*... The Government cannot concede on the principle that is
at stake here ...*[8]

... Hunger-striking, when taken to the death, has a sublime quality about it; in conjunction with terrorism it offers a consummation of murder and self-sacrifice which in a sense can legitimise the violence which precedes and follows it. If after killing – or sharing in a conspiracy to kill – for a cause one shows oneself willing to die for the same cause, a value which is adduced is higher than that of life itself ...[9]

... I don't talk to the associates of murderers ...[10]

... No special consideration is the British line. For God's sake, has not everything in the last decade been special?[11]

... We haven't won, but we're not beat yet ...[12]

... There are legends which have the patron saint of Ireland, St Patrick, hunger-striking against God. God always caved in – capitulation in the face of such self-sacrifice being seen by early Christians as a godly quality ...[13]

... it is one of the alarming characteristics of all too many Catholics these days that they seem ready to excuse terrorism or terrorists where those involved are fellow Catholics ...[14]

... The Catholic who is not a revolutionary is living in mortal sin ...[15]

... The prisons had been symbolic in the Irish Republican psyche throughout the twentieth century ...[16]

... We were not just comrades, we were blanket men ...[17]

*　　　*　　　*

On Station Island the great penance is the staying awake. There are kinder vigils on other Irish pilgrimages, where to nod off with an ear to the holy ground of the saint's bed is to be blessed, and the pilgrim is greeted on waking with the delighted congratulations of the other watchers. But neither the achievement of making it through the walking vigil nor the blessedness of a right sleep await Heaney as he does his imagined, haunted station of the night. There is only the one night for him on this island, and he spends it in the 'black dorm' of waking nightmare. He has walked out of yet another part of the 'official' pilgrimage.

The voice of the hunger-striker speaks to him out of that blackness. Without context. Unnannounced. His is the long drought of fifty-nine days' starvation, when even water became impossible to keep down:

> My brain dried like spread turf, my stomach
> Shrank to a cinder and tightened and cracked.

This is the unbearable ultimate in the alliance of violence with passivity. This is the hard-line end of 'devotion', where the extremes of religious asceticism and of armed revolution meet. This is a readiness to 'die for the cause', not just in the heat of battle or even the firing squad, but in a long-drawn-out *in*action. This is non-violent protest – by men convicted of violent acts – that becomes, inexorably, day by painful day, terminal violence against themselves.

They did not, of course, expect that they would die – not Bobby Sands, nor any others of the ten who volunteered in succession through that spring and summer of 1981, and took their strike to its unyielding conclusion in the face of an unyielding British Prime Minister. Guerrilla action in the open, and non-co-operation in the prisons: the desperate resorts of the oppressed in more countries than Ireland. In both these methods of 'resistance' Ireland has, in fact, throughout the twentieth century, given models to the world's oppressed. But in Ireland itself the situation is far too close to home: too close for Britain to see it clearly at all, and, in a wholly different way, too close to Heaney.

Although Francis Hughes died in Long Kesh, which is close to Belfast, he exists – in the thought, word and deed that the poet grants him – entirely in the intricate, secretive countryside of East Derry's lakeland that all three men grew up in: McCartney, Hughes, Heaney. There are no soft scythings in *these* meadows now, for Heaney any more than for the two that are dead, no morning dew. The grass is tracked instead with Hughes' own blood, and there is no moisture left to wash the blood and roadside muck from McCartney's eyes. In the distance the small towns – no more than hamlets by English standards – are lit up by the flashes of bombs.

In the introversion of self-starvation, its narrowing trodden circle unto death, Francis Hughes (in Heaney's dramatisation) relives on his own small territory fragments from his life as Irish Republican soldier, explosives expert and blanket-man. His living, his dying and his funeral are jumbled together in the past tenses of his telling. He was wounded and bloody, crawling again through the fields between Maghera and Glenshane where he left a blood trail that the army tracker dog picked up. His memory of wearing 'the blanket', playing his naked part in that grim H-block protest against wearing prison uniform,[18] is set in the 'ambush stillness' of lying low in familiar country. His extraordinary final journey home, when the police kept commandeering the hearse from family and friends on the long route from Long Kesh to Bellaghy, holds an image of him both as 'white-faced groom' and as hit-man:

> '... When the police yielded my coffin, I was light
> As my head when I took aim.'[19]

The images of his telescoped narrative half-resonate with images from Christ's passion: the bloody trail of the way to Calvary, the draped blanket of mockery. 'After all, they taught people to imitate Christ, so the Church can hardly complain when they go out and do just that,' said Father

Dennis Faul, the priest who worked tirelessly for the rights of the prisoners, though he was against the 1981 hunger-strike in the end.

But there is no Christian consolation here, nor pagan either. This groom is no 'bridegroom to the goddess' any more than he is a pleasing offering to the Father; he brings his people no 'germination' through his sacrifice.[20] His muddled speech is heard by the pilgrim as a voice 'from blight / And hunger', and a voice that itself dies away. And isn't that very word 'blight' blighted – in Ireland's long memory for griefs – with memories of the disease that brought about the potato famine of the 1840s, an *un*chosen mass-starvation that was still (just) in living memory when my mother was a child?

And the bog, that should be a wet and bottomless centre of fructification and preserving, does not, in the pilgrim's vision, 'work' this victim 'to a saint's kept body'. No. It is a place where 'only helicopters and curlews / Make their maimed music'. The 'medicinal repose' it offers, its ancient ways of healing, and of staunching wounds, have not been taken. There are no 'rushes that shoot green again' here, as they did at the end of Heaney's elegy for Colm McCartney, 'The Strand at Lough Beg'.

At the heart of these aching discords is the pilgrim's own sight of Hughes – not walking his purgatory like the rest of the ghosts, but dead even in the afterworld. He is only a voice, and that a dying one. And in the vision of his laying out is the final paradox:

> There he was, laid out with a drift of mass cards
> At his shrouded feet. Then the firing party's
> Volley in the yard.

In death, the appallingly shrunken body belongs both to the Catholic Church and to the Provisional IRA, though the leaders of neither organisation gave full and unequivocal support to the hunger-strike he and the rest embarked on in life. These are the tokens of their own people's recognition: the cards are earnests of Masses that will be said for the repose of Hughes' soul – a repose that Heaney cannot visualise for him at all; the volley of shots is fired over his pathetically light coffin as the final honour paid to a dead soldier of the Irish Republican Army. There would have been, too, the green, white and gold of the Irish tricolour draped over the coffin, though the Government, and indeed most of the people, of the Republic of Ireland – the twenty-six counties – would never have claimed him for their own.

Francis Hughes' body lies in Bellaghy's churchyard now, whether quietly or unquietly. In imagining a quite different burial for him, Heaney takes him out of all such political, religious and family contexts and tries to fit him into a setting that is older and more elemental: the very land of Ireland, and the stretch of particular *terra* that he and Hughes and McCartney shared.

That eastern fastness of County Derry is only forty miles west of Belfast, but it is a world apart – an unshowy flat country of small farmholdings, gravel pits, and the occasional crumbling demesne wall. But it borders Ulster's watery *omphalos*, the huge, mysterious inland sea of Lough Neagh, and is reputedly the most anciently settled part of Ireland: traces of hunter-fishers have been found near here dating back eight or nine thousand years. At the lough's northern mouth, the great fish-weirs of their descendents still tease the waters of the Bann river as it flows on to form the 'small lough', Lough Beg. The A6 from Belfast to Derry hammers overhead regardless through the bridge village of Toome – the name is from the Gaelic *tuama*, 'tumulus'.

And its tradition of rural Republicanism is still touched with the 'simplicity of mind and directness of purpose' of the 1916 ideal[21] – a simplicity and directness that may paradoxically have helped Hughes and his fellow striker from Bellaghy to cope with the mounting psychological pressures of the hunger-strike.

Heaney travels in spirit to the intimate and layered landscape all these men hold in common. But the buildings

he sees there in his vision are worm-eaten; there is a smell
of mildew in 'the byre loft where [Hughes] watched and
hid'. This ancient country, this heartland that Heaney has
returned and returned to for images of regeneration, is
stained now with rot. The new 'Troubles' of the North have
exacerbated the loneliness and the waste, the narrowing
down of choices in the ghetto of nationalist commitment.[22]
What, now, does 'community' mean? And where shall
renewal, the 'dearest freshness deep down things', be
sought, if the *omphalos*, the bottomless wet centre, is itself
polluted?

*   *   *

Heaney's nightmare carries him on from reportage and
failed admonition to the grimmest of his station's
emblematic visions, the very one that haunted me, months
before, when I first gazed into the waters of Lough Derg.
Against Hughes' passionate certainty, both in his active
service and in his dying, against his closed and
self-absorbed witness, Heaney places his own 'softly awash
and blanching self-disgust', and cries out his own version
of the Renunciations:

> I repent
> My unweaned life that kept me competent
> To sleepwalk with connivance and mistrust.

Harangue, reproach, accusation – he has taken a mounting
battery from his ghosts. He has no guide to mediate
between him and the shades he summons, or to moderate
his own ventriloquism. Who, after all, puts these
accusations into their mouths but himself? On this retreat
there is no spiritual director. Heaney is cut off from the
support of family, friends, colleagues – and Mother Church.
He is plain, unaccommodated man. He is only himself, and

adrift even from that.

The horror bred by the extremes of the hunger-striker's death and his own 'unweaned life' is expressed in an image of beauty and nourishment destroyed:

All seemed to run to waste
As down a swirl of mucky, glittering flood
Strange polyp floated like a huge corrupt
Magnolia bloom, surreal as a shed breast.

Here is dislocation from the most elemental symbols of the feminine. The waters are muddied. Tumour, rot and mastectomy crowd out the memory of 'the granaries of words like *breasts*'. It is his own self-disgust that has been keeping him in a state of infantile and unhealthy dependence.

The Saint Patrick's Purgatory pilgrimage preserves to this day the pattern of an ancient rite of death and rebirth. Somehow, the poet needs not just to be 'reborn of water and the holy spirit' in some mystic baptism or washing-clean that is beyond or beneath the conventions of his Catholic upbringing: he must also be weaned – a second weaning? – into a new understanding and acceptance of the passivity he has grown to despise: the shadow side of Wordsworth's 'wise passiveness',[23] just as the sleepwalking 'with connivance and mistrust' is the shadow side of the 'somnambulist encounter' that listens out for poems.

And even if he can make peace with the feminine within himself and his people – an outcome still uncertain – what is he to make of the masculine? Does a Catholic upbringing in the North of Ireland force one for ever into the extremes of connivance or kicking over the traces, of playing for ever versions of victim or killer? Polly Devlin, who grew up on the Lough shore just a few miles south of Heaney, has written of the 'self-hatred and dolourousness that poisons so many of the lives around us', and tries to explain it.

The loyalties and the love we feel towards our

putative nation and powerful religion are subversive.
Loyalty towards the idea of Ireland and love for
Mother Church are inextricably tangled, yet neither
religion nor country has status, official sanction or
respect. The feelings we have or cultivate for these
important influences in our lives are something akin to
the love we feel for the women around us – protective,
fierce, yet contemptuous, because they are not
powerful, and not respected or even recognised by the
powers that we know to be.[24]

In Poems VII, VIII and IX, Heaney meets the ghosts of men
who have tried to *be* men within this constricting and
still-colonised community. He finds little comfort, or pattern
for the future, in their lives. And they have scarcely
acknowledged *his* rôle as poet, and poet of his people,
except by attacking it. Where is he to find affirmation and
illumination now, as human being, as poet, as man?

The possibility – the promise? – of a mystical re-
integration of masculine and feminine appears briefly and
emblematically from out of the very vision of corruption
which has made the pilgrim cry out his words of
self-disgust. The strange polyp puts forth the dreamlike
growth of a lighted candle. It rises up 'like a pistil', that is,
like the female, seed-receiving organ of a flower; but it is
also erect and purposeful, able to retrieve a course and to
respond to and reveal the currents of the waters that it
'rides'.

So strange and surreal a vision! And yet – hasn't another
Irish poet written of a vision of a white breast on a watery
flood, a vision, too, that offers him a way of reconciling the
dead with the living? That it is the feathered breast of a
bird and not of a woman hardly diminishes its charge. In
'Downstream', Thomas Kinsella, using Dantean *terza rima*,
tells of a night river-journey in a skiff towards the site of
the ancient monastery of Durrow. The remembered story of
a man's rotting corpse in the riverbank bushes takes the
rowers into a sort of hell,

> to the evil dream where rodents ply,
> Man-rumped, sow-headed, busy with whip and maul

> Among nude herds of the damned.

Kinsella's nightmare is filled, not with dead friends, but with the smell of the rumoured body in the bushes, and with the dead of the distant war in Europe, from which Ireland was even then holding aloof in her neutrality.[25] The current suddenly takes hold of the boat and speeds it terrifyingly towards the Mill Hole – 'the abyss'.

> We shipped our oars in dread. Now, deeper in,

> Something shifted in sleep, a quiet hiss
> As we slipped by. Adrift . . . A milk-white
> > breast . . .
> A shuffle of wings betrayed with a feathery kiss

> A soul of white with darkness for a nest.

For Kinsella, a bird's whiteness in the darkest place, for Heaney a rotting bloom like a shed breast that grows a lit candle from its centre: for both poets, an emblematic way out of nightmare. In 'Downstream', the stars 'occupied their stations and descended':

> The slow, downstreaming dead, it seemed, were blended
> One with those silver hordes, and briefly shared
> Their order, glittering.

But Kinsella's voyage is nearly over. His boat party is 'Searching the darkness for a landing place'. Heaney is only three-quarters of the way through *his* pilgrimage, and just about everything remains, jaggy and intractable still, to be resolved.

*   *   *

I hear the dawn begin with the sleepy cries of gulls. This lake is not *aornos* the 'birdless' place, like Avernus, Italy's more famous entrance to the underworld. Somewhere, out of sight over dark water, a colony of gulls is stirring. They call and answer in harsh and sporadic couplets. Then they begin to sweep into visibility overhead as the darkness thins. How gradually the dawn comes this far north . . .

At last – a gleam below the overcast. The sun has risen, somewhere, behind thick cloud. The bell calls us once more into the basilica. We have made it right through the long night to morning Mass.

'Aren't we great?' says Thérèse. Nuala nods with an eagerness wrested from exhaustion. '*It* was great – the vigil – just to have got through it. I feel good – and then again, I feel – just *dreadful!*'

We laugh. But Billy doesn't. 'Well, I think it was barbarous. I just can't think what it's . . . What *does* it . . . ? Oh – I just wish I hadn't come!'

'Billy . . .' the women remonstrate.

'I suppose it's an experience, and part of Irish spirituality, and all that. But it doesn't seem to have anything to do with me – or my faith – or *anything.*'

Round us now the third-day pilgrims gather, spilling from the hostel dormitories, pink and surprised from sleep. Everyone seems to be smiling – even the second-day pilgrims like us who are wan from the vigil. Everyone except Billy. And me. The air is full of murmured congratulations and thanks-be's. The 'kindness of the island' is there to put us together again, to lap all our separateness and anguish of the night watches into a communal happy ending. I don't know what lies behind Billy's inability to join in; neither then nor later is he able – or free – to articulate his distress to me. Thérèse, who was responsible for bringing him to the island, hurries him inside now to Mass. But I know that I, too, for my own reasons, cannot take to heart the 'release' the island offers; I jib at its structured joy.

The ghosts that I have met on the night watch, both

Heaney's and my own, rise up from lives and situations too complex for such sugared solutions, however interim or temporary those solutions claim to be. So what are we all here for? Just to win a brief and illusory respite from the real-life pain of difficulty by giving mind and body a paced and circumscribed 'difficult' task? Is it so that we can get a spurious sense of achievement, or even just the plain relief of contrast? I have a sinking feeling that on the island all confusions have an 'explanation', that pain can be magically defused by being pigeon-holed, and 'shared'. That way of thought does not seem a possible part of the messy and adult world I am exiled to. I am cut off for ever from the Catholic – and particularly Irish Catholic – optimism that is being visibly generated around me. From some exiles there is no return.

I wonder to what extent it has really worked for my fellow pilgrims, but can only guess at the griefs and troubles that lie beneath the cheery smiles of their 'we have come through'. I am left with my own, and the night has put salt, not wine and honey, into the wounds.

I grew up with a simple nationalism, as I did with a simple Catholicism. 'When I was a child, I used to talk like a child, and think as a child …' But I have grown up now, I have borne children of my own. Like so many of Ireland's children, I have been forced into living in another country. Yet all I can see now at the centre of both my native creeds is a travesty of nurturing: the denial of the very giving of life. I cannot quickly put from my mind the death of Francis Hughes. But my own nightmare vision – hanging over still from the Night Vigil – is of a baroque *pietà*, a marble mother holding a dead son in her arms. And as voice-over I hear part of the graveside oration given by Owen Carron when Bobby Sands, the first hunger-striker to die, was buried in Belfast's Milltown cemetery:

Someone once said it is hard to be a hero's mother
and nobody knows that better than Mrs Sands who
watched her son being daily crucified and tortured for

sixty-six long days and eventually killed. Mrs Sands epitomises the Irish mothers who in every generation watched their children go out and die for freedom.[26]

There is no doubting the individual, the community pain. But this icon of a passive and anguished un-mothering is no fitting emblem of adversity for either nationalism or Christianity now. A worn circle is trodden, decade after terrible decade, with a disastrous limp that pulls away from self-knowledge, and into a cult of death.

In Heaney's 'Station Island' there is not even the cold comfort of a funeral scene like this version of Sands' to mark the death of Francis Hughes. No women are raising the keen for him, not as Heaney tells it. From Heaney's station, it is not just the god who 'has, as they say, withdrawn'. The goddess, too, has departed.

When, in *Preoccupations*,[27] Heaney wrote about Ireland's 'indigenous territorial numen, a tutelar of the whole island', he went on to give some of her traditional names:

... call her Mother Ireland, Kathleen Ni Houlihan, the poor old woman, the Shan Van Vocht, whatever ...

It's an image that dates back at least as far as the tough days of the Penal Laws: 'I am her prisoner – but she too is a prisoner' sang Ó Rathaille in his most powerful *aisling* lovesong and lament.[28]

In 'Station Island', set ten years after that *Preoccupations* essay, this is part of the absence of the feminine that has intrigued and summoned me. And there is an absence of comment, too. When the young priest in the fourth poem utters that wan statement, 'The god has, as they say, withdrawn', he does not go on to say whether 'they' have hazarded anything about the goddess. Nor does Heaney articulate her withdrawal elsewhere in his text, though her elusive representatives move silently in the corner of the text's eye.

Centre-stage, however – in political and religious life,

and in Heaney's 'Station Island' autobiography – are men who in their different ways might all be said to be followers of the goddess as territorial and religious numen. They are native Irish, nationalists, Catholics. (Catholicism is, after all, a religion with far more of the feminine articulated within it than Protestantism, for all my strictures on it.) But neither in old nor in new-fangled ways is her presence marked by them. Rather, the men themselves seem caught in the tragic and victimised attitudes of her least attractive personae.

Is this an inevitable consequence of being the colonised for so many centuries – the crude 'feminisation' of a people? Has the Irish consciousness been made irredeemably passive by the assertive and invasive actions of its neighbour and coloniser? Heaney certainly saw it in those classic gender terms when he wrote, after naming Ireland Mother Ireland and Kathleen Ni Houlihan, that

> her sovereignty has been temporarily usurped or
> infringed by a new male cult whose founding fathers
> were Cromwell, William of Orange and Edward
> Carson, and whose godhead is incarnate in a rex or
> caesar resident in a palace in London.[29]

But such versions of mythology ring hollow on Station Island. 'Mother Ireland' is played out, the beautiful *aisling* is turned from and forgotten. As Heaney the pilgrim meets the men of his central poems meeting their deaths, he has none of the old explanations and comforts either, no structures within which he can share their pain. He and they are left high and dry, without even the consoling lie of 'martyrdom for the sake of Kathleen Ni Houlihan'.

And what does it say to me, and to the women of Ireland, this tale told, as so often in Ireland, in the men's version? As I start, and drift in and out of consciousness all through, this second Mass, I think not at all of the scriptural readings – they float past me unheard – but of the trivial fact that Heaney's first waking action after the nightmare is shaving: he hates his 'half-composed face / In the shaving mirror'. Is it petty of me, just plain simplistic, to feel so very excluded?

And I think of the irony for the women Republican prisoners in Armagh jail who felt excluded in a very specific way: from participating in that hunger-strike of 1981. To take their place in the 'masculine' work of armed revolt, or even hunger-striking, women have to become – as far as is possible – indistinguishable from the men. This is despite the pioneering example of hunger-striking given by Irish, and then English, suffragettes.

> The attitudes of the female volunteers as soldiers first
> and foremost – reveal an identification with the
> Republican movement which is so complete that it
> precludes any awareness of their own position as
> women.[30]

In a community defined by conflict with an external opponent, as Ireland has been for so long, there is a great danger of the postponing and long-term suppression of that community and culture's self-knowledge. The marginalising of women, and so, inevitably, of any admission of the feminine within men as well as women, is an issue too often put off until after the revolution. In Irish Republican circles, this well-known tendency has, ironically, been made worse by romantic appeals to an ancient Ireland in which men and women were extraordinarily equal under the Brehon Laws.[31]

> If the subjection of Irish women was directly related to
> the foreign conquest of Ireland, then Irishmen, who
> had also suffered from foreign domination, could not
> be blamed for what had occurred over the intervening
> centuries. As they were fighting for freedom, in some
> unexpressed manner it was always assumed that they
> must be fighting for the freedom of women. In
> Republican mythology, Irish men used to be

non-oppressive and this dubious proposition somehow becomes transmuted into an assurance that they will automatically become so again – as soon as the contaminating effects of 'foreign influence' are removed.[32]

In this most ancient place of visitation, this island lapped by fresh water and given over to the sign of the circle, that specious invocation of a myth of a once and future male-female harmony seems a kind of blasphemy. It is a denial of the now we all inhabit.

NOTES

1.   Emily Dickinson, 'After great pain, a formal feeling comes –' (poem 341).
2.   The IRA claimed responsibility for my uncle's murder later the same day. As one of the very small number of Catholic judges in the Northern Ireland judiciary, he had enemies on all sides: he had, for instance, sent Ian Paisley to prison, as well as members of the IRA. He himself was sure that if he were to be assassinated it would be by the UVF, the Protestant paramilitary force. His widow was as astonished as he would have been when news of the IRA claim came through.
3.   W.B. Yeats, *The King's Threshold* (1904), *Collected Plays*, p.141. Yeats' prescient play anticipated the revival of the ancient tradition of the hunger-strike in the twentieth century Irish Republican movement.
4.   Virgil, *Aeneid*, VI, 309-10.
5.   *Dubliners*, p.255-6. Michael Furey is the long-dead sweetheart of Gabriel Conroy's wife Gretta who haunts the closing scenes of the story.
6.   Yeats, op. cit., p.108.
7.   David Beresford, *Ten Men Dead*, p.25.
8.   Humphrey Atkins, Secretary of State for Northern Ireland, 1980.
9.   Beresford, op. cit., p.38.
10.   Harold McCusker, Unionist MP for Armagh, during the 1981 hunger-strike.

11.   *Irish Times* editorial during the 1981 hunger-strike.
12.   Bobby Sands, after the 1980 hunger-strike was called off,
quoted in Beresford, op. cit., p.14.
13.   Beresford, op. cit., p.15.
14.   *Daily Mail* editorial during the 1981 hunger-strike.
15.   Camillo Torres, quoted in Beresford, op. cit.
16.   Beresford, op. cit., p.31.
17.   Ex-prisoner, Long Kesh, quoted in Beresford, op. cit., p.397.
The average age of the prisoners on the blanket was, at the height
of the protest, around twenty.
18.   It needs saying that the men and women who took part in
the 'blanket' or 'dirty protests' in the Province's prisons during
the seventies and early eighties did not come only from the
nationalist community. Many loyalist prisoners were also fighting
for political status, and used the same methods of resisting the
label 'criminal'.
19.   For an account of Francis Hughes' cortège and funeral, see
Beresford, op. cit., pp.170-4.
20.   See 'The Tollund Man', first of the 'Bog' poems inspired by
P.V. Glob's book *The Bog People*, in Heaney's *Wintering Out*
21.   These honours would still be paid to a veteran of Ireland's
original Republican Army, who had fought in the official –
though uncompleted – war of independence following the Easter
1916 Rising: a veteran such as an elderly cousin of mine who was
buried with full honours in County Galway in the mid-seventies.
But there is a very different attitude in the South to the 'Irish
Republican Army' active in Ulster during the seventies and
eighties. See Beresford, op. cit., p.152:

> Frank Hughes was fairly typical of the rural Republican
> tradition: unsophisticated in political terms, with a taste for
> cliché – 'I die in a good cause ... for mother Ireland ... that
> others may be set free ...' – which would set their urban
> contemporaries ashudder, but with a simplicity of mind and
> directness of purpose which left them largely untouched
> by the bloody, ideological schisms which repeatedly rent
> the Movement in the cities. As the clothes he was wearing
> when he was captured testified, he considered himself an
> Irish soldier and as such regarded it as a point of honour to
> wear what approximated to a uniform whenever he could.

22.   Heaney expresses his desire for an end to the tradition of fighting in the North through a characteristically rural image: a rather obscure reference to the communal behaviour of the Irish stoat, commonly called 'the weasel' there. There's a tale found throughout rural Ireland that, when a weasel dies, all its friends and relations go to the funeral. Heaney, however, makes use in addition of a more narrowly Northern tradition, that a weasel can call all his friends to his aid by putting the tip of his tail between his teeth and whistling. See James Fairley, *An Irish Beast Book*, p.166.

23.   *Preoccupations*, p.63. It is worth quoting the full context of this key phrase, since its images of centre and circling are very apposite to the Station Island pilgrimage: 'What we are presented with [in the opening lines of *The Prelude*] is a version of composition as listening, as a wise passiveness, a surrender to energies that spring within the centre of the mind, not composition as an active pursuit by the mind's circumference of something already at the centre.'

24.   *All of Us There*, p.161. Polly Devlin is the sister of Heaney's wife Marie.

25.   'Downstream' (in the collection of the same name) is set in the same contentious period of Ireland's Second World War neutrality as Patrick Kavanagh's *Lough Derg*. See also 'Downstream II', the revised version, in *The Penguin Book of Irish Verse* edited by Brendan Kennelly.

26.   John M. Feehan, *Bobby Sands and the Tragedy of Northern Ireland*, p.19.

27.   *Preoccupations*, p.57. Yeats' play *Cathleen ni Houlihan* brings her to strong and spirited life. Robert Welch writes illuminatingly of the way in which the play transforms the everyday rural setting it starts from:

> The naturalistic, homely convention is held right up to the point at which the old woman begins to intone the names of Ireland's dead. At that point the audience realises she is other. At that point, too, all the old identifications of Ireland with a female figure, stretching right back to the goddess of sovereignty herself in Celtic mythology, are reactivated and *because* the naturalistic convention has been so definitely established the old networks of emotion are given locality and actuality. (*Irish Writers and the Theatre* edited by

Masaru Sekine, Irish Literary Studies 23, p.213.)
28.   *An Duanaire*, pp.150-1. Ó Rathaille lived from c.1675 to
1729. Ó Tuama and Kinsella say in a note on his poems: 'His
poetry, the best of which has a heroic desolation and grandeur,
is in many ways a result of his effort to come to terms with the
chaos in which he and his people found themselves.'
29.   *Preoccupations*, p.57.
30.   See *Unmanageable Revolutionaries* by Margaret Ward, p.260,
and her account of contemporary Republican attitudes on pp.254-
63. The rest of her book gives a depressing account of the ways
in which, because of both external opposition and internal
division between feminists and nationalists, women have
consistently been excluded from positions of influence in
Ireland's political history during the last hundred years. But the
incompatibility of nationalism and the liberation of women is not
just Ireland's problem: 'Nationalist movements do not liberate
women as such because national freedom is identified with male
freedom.' Mary Daly, *Beyond God the Father*, p.54. ·
31.   See *Sex and Marriage in Ancient Ireland* by Patrick C. Power,
passim.
32.   Ward, op. cit., pp.254-5.

CHAPTER ELEVEN

A Mug to Hold Spring Water

Poems IX & X

Monday 3 August 1987: morning
The Sacrament of Reconciliation

> I wake to sleep, and take my waking slow.
> I learn by going where I have to go.
>
> Theodore Roethke

Kitchen dresser in Co. Down, after a photograph by Robert John Welch

'And now,' says the priest from the lectern near the altar, 'we come to the central sacrament of the pilgrimage: the Sacrament of Reconciliation.'

For a moment I am baffled, until I remember that what he's talking about is 'Confession'. Then I begin to panic. Morning Mass is over. All the third-day pilgrims have just been given their Papal Blessing, and have hurried out to make their final station round the basilica and the beds, before catching the boats to the mainland and home. I am unequivocally a second-dayer, caught up, with no chance of escape, in the machinery of the sacrament. Already ten or twelve priests have gone to the front and sides of the basilica. Each pew-ful of pilgrims is being advised which of them to queue for. My pew is directed towards the three priests spread out along the left half of the altar-rail. Under the new dispensation, each individual's confession will be made in everyone's sight, though whispered to avoid being in their hearing. So there is not even the dark of the confessional to hide my confusion!

Unless I feign illness – a dizzy spell? – I will have to take my turn. From schooldays I dredge up strategies for fainting: putting wet Kleenex 'insoles' in one's shoes before morning Mass . . . (it looks as though my row will be one of the first to go forward) . . . holding one's breath whilst saying a whole Creed and Gloria, slowly . . . (our half of the pew is motioned to stand in the central aisle) . . . poking a finger behind the elastic of one's veil and twisting it round and round until it tightens on the head . . . (there are only three people in front of me, and there are three priests to go to) . . . simply *acting* a faint . . .[1]

It's no good. It's too late to manufacture a real faint, and my acting skills for that sort of thing are limited. I'll just have to blather my way through.

'Bless me, Father, for I have sinned.

'It is nineteen years since my last confession.' A sharp intake of breath. Then he speaks to me very gently, very kindly. Am I the lost sheep that he will lift up from the thorn thicket of the lapsed, and carry back to the herd this day? But out of all those nineteen years there is only one thing I can think of that troubles me in relation to the faith I grew up in.

'Last month, Father, my divorce came through.'

In the South of Ireland, of course, divorce is not allowed by Church *or* state – if you can distinguish the two on this matter. My divorce took place in England, as did my marriage twenty years before. The state made no objections. The Church wasn't asked. Over there it seemed just our business.

Ken and I were breaking up, I realise, during the very season in which Heaney sets his pilgrimage, the summer of 1984. I found myself then and for months, years, on a Station Island of the mind: stripped down, distracted, and haunted by the past. Like the pilgrim Heaney in whatever dislocation he faced that summer, I instinctively went right back into my childhood in an attempt to understand the disaster, and my self. At that time, I found only partial explanations for my biddableness, my 'offer it up' mentality. Now, they come more clearly. I realise that, despite all our intentions of egality, I brought my Catholic and Irish and female reflexes of selflessness into the marriage right from its start. As if being a woman wasn't enough of a handicap, I was an Irish and a Catholic woman through and through, never mind my moving to England, never mind my 'lapse' into agnosticism, just one year after the wedding.

It was my struggles, much later, to move on from repining self-denial to a willed self-centring that revealed how unworkable for me was a marriage based on such a past. Late, late in the day, I had to learn to live in the open.

'The symbol for shock, imbalance, break-up is being cast out, forced into seclusion or into the wilderness, plunged into darkness, exile, blindfolded. It is a symbolism offered in ritual,' says Bani Shorter, in her study[2] of the ways women instinctively create rituals of their own to mark stages in their life's journey towards meaning. Like so many, I made that journey outside the structures of any church. Though it was all about aloneness, I made parts of it in the company of friends – mainly, though not all, women – and in the love of my daughters. I felt only a very little wiser, more experienced, than my daughters, as they entered their teens. So very much to learn, and so late a start. Why? Because of my religion? Because of the whole generation I was born into?

Now, in this basilica, lapped once again in the formal rituals of my cradle and marriage-bed faith, a great sadness comes over me. I need to make peace with the self who made those wedding vows twenty years before in the conviction that they were indissoluble. I cannot deny that nineteen-year-old her own autonomy, unwish her convictions. Nor can I dismiss those chosen years of marriage, even though the state of marriage is an irrelevance to the me that has come through, and an irrelevance to Michael. Ken and I have unsaid our vows; our present and our future have nothing directly to do with each other any more. But he is the man I called – as I shall never now call another – 'husband', the man with whom I made a family under that old dispensation. Nothing of that can be unmade – the facts, the love, the years. I do not want, now that the pain and anger of our parting has subsided, to be a revisionist autobiographer. We cannot afford to jettison such acres of ourselves, of our pasts.

And there is still more to come to terms with: this religion that we both grew up in. Did I really not know what I was doing when I came here on a supposedly literary quest? Kneeling at the altar-rail in the basilica, I reflect that perhaps to come this far and step in this deep, has been crazy.

'And is there anything else, my child?' the priest prompts gently, calling me back from that past.

'That's all, Father.'

'You're quite sure?' (A little plaintively. I've let him down properly.)

Oh yes, quite sure. I'm sorry to disappoint the poor man, but my divorce is the only act of my life that is still remotely the Church's business. Not that I want to explain it or apologise for it: I speak its name under this roof as a sort of exorcism. And I certainly don't tell him I've been living for over a year with Michael. *He* would call that 'living in sin'. For us it has been our own continuing and unfinished sacrament of reconciliation, after the break-ups and pile-ups of the middle part of each of our lives.

But there is also reconciliation for me here, in this church and Church. Suddenly I feel good. With my short but far-reaching 'confession' I have made some sort of peace between my old religion and my self. And I feel, for the first time on the island, free of anxiety and its projection, anger. A last binding of guilt, a last apron-string of Mother Church, falls to the ground.

I would like to sleep now, for my soul's healing as well as in response to my body's crying need. I remember with fondness the vigil I made on a tiny salt-water island off Ireland's west coast three summers ago, the very summer when my marriage was breaking apart. It was the vigil of the patron saint's day, his 'pattern day'. I stayed overnight in the tiny stone hut that is built over the saint's bed – in this instance a grave slab of great antiquity – with three of the island women. They said endless rosaries in Irish, and every so often one in English, in case I should feel left out.

'Sure Our Blessed Lady and Saint Cavan will grant you your intention.' I hear Mairead's soft voice as I sit upright with a jerk, awake . . . But I am not in the candle- and breath-warmed hut on Inisheer. I am sitting on a slippery wooden bench at the back of Saint Patrick's basilica on Station Island, where I have come to say the prayers of penance my confessor gave me.

Is it any wonder that the prior has just warned us not to lie down, even on grass or flagstones in the open air, on this, our difficult, tedious second day? Sleep is to be our enemy for some hours yet – until ten o'clock this evening, to be precise. Even sitting upright I am not safe from it. This relentless fight against sleep is from a harsh tradition of asceticism that I do not naturally incline to, in theory any

more than in practice. Closer to my heart is that pattern of
Inisheer, with its tradition of self-healing that has 'ancient
roots in the ritual practices of incubation and initiation.'[3]
For I remember my body's wisdom, its instinctive gift of
sedation, when I slept such long nights, and half the days,
in the initial shock of my husband's sudden leaving.

But my mood is milder now, less critical. I will attempt
to keep to the Lough Derg rules. I am even curious to see
what effects such continuing privations may have on me in
the twenty-four hours that remain.

*   *   *

Shriven and thoughtful, we second-dayers all emerge, in
twos and threes, into the open air once more, and I think
with wry resentment that Heaney's pilgrim persona has
skipped all this. Just as he stepped out of the basilica and
the evening Mass in his sixth poem, he has 'pitched
backwards in a headlong fall' in his ninth, and woken
twenty-four hours ahead of me

> To sunlight and a bell and gushing taps
> In the next cubicle.

But Heaney cannot, of course, step out of his own skin, or
out of his upbringing. Both nature and nurture hang on to
us all for grim death:

> As if the eddy could transform the pool.
> As if a stone swirled under a cascade,
> Eroded and eroding in its bed,
> Could grind itself down to a different core.

The ghost he faces now is himself.

Back at the water's edge, before night fell, the
mirror-surface of the lake had yielded nothing, no reflection

of himself any more than of his dead friend. Now, the
non-mystic, everyday, sunlit shaving mirror shows him his
'half-composed face'. And the sight of it moves him to a
spirited and wide-ranging expression of hatred:

> I hate how quick I was to know my place.
> I hate where I was born, hate everything
> That made me biddable and unforthcoming, ...

But it is not a simple self-hatred, nor even a 'slow distaste'.[4]
Heaney sees himself as a drunken man who has escaped
into the bathroom at a party, a man who is 'lulled' as well
as 'repelled by his own reflection'. *In vino veritas*? Or is it
the sudden solitude, the withdrawal from 'the party'?
Whatever prompts it, there is a growing note of
self-acceptance, self-forgiveness, even *reconciliation* here. The
'as ifs' of those stone and water images become ambiguous:
they simultaneously deny and suggest the possibility of
transformation.

   This matted and painful ninth poem began in drought
and blight, and with a wounded man remembering the
dogs on his own blood-trail. It finishes with two lines that
evoke a different sort of hunt, and one that offers a first
movement away from passivity (and away from Ireland?):

> Then I thought of the tribe whose dances never fail
> For they keep dancing till they sight the deer.

Sketched in, slipped in – a moment from the prelapsarian,
'primitive' world of the hunter-gatherer, in which hunter
and quarry are drawn together by need, and by dance, and
by perseverance.

   It's only a flicker – but it could be the second inkling
that, against all the grim instances of masculine excess and
feminine withdrawal witnessed on Heaney's island, the
pilgrim is at last going to offer some paradigm of the
positive. Will he? And will there be, in the concluding,
waking, poems of his sequence some more positive

presence of the feminine in particular?

*   *   *

I'm having trouble with Heaney's tenth poem. Is it because he has skipped to one whole day ahead of me? *He* is preparing his pilgrim self for departure while *I* am, wearily, less than halfway through my time on the island – and I haven't (officially) been to sleep yet. Has my own 'sacrament of reconciliation' put me out of tune with the movement of his sequence? Am I too eager for a continuation of his autobiographical sub-plot now, after all his engagement in the lives (and deaths) of other men during the last three poems? My own experience of leaving part of my 'childhood' behind during my confession has made me hungry for the pilgrim Heaney to move on into the grown-up world.

Are my expectations misguided, too centred on self – or is there something out of kilter within the very argument of his poem? This moment in the sequence should be a turning-point, I think, a beginning of the return to a lived and livable life. After the land of Death, a kind of rebirth: Lough Derg's ritual pattern which is older than Catholicism, older than any sect of Christianity. But I cannot quite follow why it is that here, at this point in the sequence, the pilgrim goes back so literally to the world of childhood – almost to the indoor time of infancy suggested in the third poem.

'Morning stir in the hostel.' The grown-up images of shaving and party-going in the latter lines of Poem IX are far away. The pilgrim is at an archetypal rural hearth, a place where hearthsmoke and sunlight from the open door mingle. Mossbawn, perhaps? At any rate, a first world where the hearth is the true *focus* of home, and the household gods (Heaney even uses the Roman word *lars*) can inhabit material and secular forms. (There is no mention of the 'official' icon of the Sacred Heart on *this* kitchen wall.)

> Hearthsmoke rambling and a thud of earthenware

> drumming me back until I saw the mug
> beyond my reach on its high shelf ...

And thus the chief subject of the poem is introduced: artefact, ornament, vessel. This mug is itself and more than itself in its epiphany. It contains, 'in its patient sheen and turbulent atoms', both stillness and movement. Although its earthenware is, from a Newtonian viewpoint, a piece of 'patient' and unmoving matter, the sprigs on its surface circle and circle the mug with a paradoxical sense of journey, 'blue sprig after sprig / repeating round it, as quiet as a milestone' – a milestone, the physical marker of travel that is yet utterly still in itself. The sprigs' circling seems to enact the clay's inner memory of the potter's wheel, where its 'turbulent atoms' were once centred and raised; just as, from the turbulent atoms of the past, memory, and poetry the child of memory, raise up a vessel from the forgotten. And all the other circuits of the 'Station Island' sequence, both the confining and the enabling ones, find an echo in its thrown and fired circularity. Does this simple vessel, then, made within one of humanity's oldest technologies, offer a positive pattern – that of tensions held in balance and stillness?

It was not a mug for use, however – or for *child*-use, at any rate. Its blue and white was part of the display of delftware that was the traditional Irish kitchen's proud centrepiece, its dresserful[5] of 'delf'. Suddenly it strikes me as odd that so recognisable a scene lacks its key inhabitant – the one who tends the hearth. This is the very withindoors that Padraic Colum's old woman of the roads longed for when she dreamt of 'fixing on their shelf again / [her] white and blue and speckled store.'[6] And the first of Heaney's own dedicatory poems in *North* is set in just such

a room. There his aunt, Mary Heaney, is indoors from the
sunlit farmyard and at the reddening stove, baking.

> Now she dusts the board
> with a goose's wing,
> now sits, broad-lapped,
> with whitened nails
>
> and measling shins:
> here is a space
> again, the scone rising
> to the tick of two clocks.
>
> And here is love
> like a tinsmith's scoop
> sunk past its gleam
> in the meal-bin.

But at the hearth of this later poem, Heaney, as child and
as pilgrim, is alone – and there is not even a sense of the
absence of another. This is what jars, suddenly: the absence
of absence.

I'm still hoping that love, and nourishment, and the
growing world – all so unwritten-of since the radiant sixth
poem – will re-enter the sequence, and become once more
part of its 'argument'. In this poem the theme of courtship
returns, but with what indirectness and distressing
distance! Apart from one reference in Poem VII to a
younger, slimmer Heaney 'courting in that big Austin ... on
a Sunday night', the under-plot of autobiography has taken
its story no further. So lovers are present here, yes, and
welcome – except that they are fictional and thin, and seen
by the quirky and 'innocent' eye of the child.

For the vision of the mug starts off a further memory:
the story of its safe return from an evening of make-believe
and estrangement, away from hearth and home. It was once
borrowed as a prop by 'fit-up' actors – the sort of troupe
that tours from hall to village hall up and down rural

Ireland, like Brian Friel's faith healer,[7] and works its own brand of miracle, its own suspensions of disbelief. 'I sat in a dark hall estranged from it,' remembers the child who is now a grown man,

> as a couple vowed and called it their loving cup

> and held it in our gaze until the curtain
> jerked shut with an ordinary noise.

Poem VI, with its closing image of entering 'the land of kindness', suggested a consummation both literal and metaphorical, even a marriage; but its story seems now, from this distance, to have the insulting half-truth of a happy-ever-after ending. The narrative of 'after' has played no part in the relentlessly masculine story-line of the poems since, and now, when its theme returns, the plot is stuck at the same point, that high point of courtship's end – but how thin it has become, how much less radiant and true its indistinct 'couple'. The woman of Poem VI still withholds her face. In retrospect I find shocking her status as looked-at and unlooking object. If she is never to turn round, what am I to make of her frozen icon?

The icon of *this* poem is the flowered mug: it too suffers no visible alteration. Should I be glad? I am not sure. It is returned 'with all its cornflower haze / still dozing, its parchment glazes fast'. But something troubling has happened to change it in some invisible way: it is 'Dipped and glamoured from this translation'. *Glamoured*? Something magical, something beyond the laws of nature, has occurred.

I can remember, as a child, that I was confused when I went to plays and films, not so much between fiction and real life, as between these secular dramas and the utterly familiar sacred drama of the Mass. I always got into trouble with my brother for genuflecting as I stepped into the cinema's central aisle after Saturday morning cartoon programmes down on the Lisburn Road. 'Get up!' he'd hiss urgently. 'They'll know you're a Catholic!'

Did the child Heaney have something of the same confusion, I wonder, when he gazed at his mug – his mug become a 'loving cup', and held up like the chalice elevated in the sight of the faithful at the Consecration of the Mass? Why has Heaney the poet fixed his returning gaze on so ambivalent a drinking vessel?

And with the long-drawn-out and formal simile that ends the poem, my confusion deepens. For the poet suddenly takes us back into the world of Sweeney, that first world of Ireland so reluctantly abandoned in Poem I, but he now appears to have taken sides with Sweeney's chief oppressor. The poem steps through the 'open door letting in sunlight', into the outdoors and into that incident from the very beginning of Sweeney's mythic conflict with Christianity:

> ... its parchment glazes fast –
> as the otter surfaced once with Ronan's psalter
> miraculously unharmed, that had been lost
> a day and a night under lough water.

And so the saint praised God on the lough shore.

Ronan the implacable cleric comes on as a nice guy, and God – who had, 'as they say, withdrawn' (Poem IV) – even gets His capital letter back. Is this a wholly unexpected sacrament of reconciliation – a generous forgiving of Ronan? Or is it a laundering? In this outdoors the naked, desperate figure of Sweeney, the man who threw the psalter into the lough, is nowhere. Unmentioned. Heaney, who has elsewhere identified so closely with the distracted poet-king, seems at variance even with himself. He can't really be on Ronan's side over this, can he?

I hold on to the untrustworthiness of 'glamour' in its original meanings of 'enchantment' and 'delusive charm'. And grasp at the unpleasant connotations of the words 'dazzle' and 'glare'.[8] For, after the psalter's safe return:

The dazzle of the impossible suddenly
blazed across the threshold, a sun-glare
to put out the small hearths of constancy.

Both restorations – of the mug and of the psalter – are
fraught with uncomfortable ambiguities, confused
messages. Is it *good* that the 'small hearths of constancy'
should be put out? Are miracles and magic to be welcomed,
or is it in the ordinary that we shall find ourselves? Is a
miracle a moment of epiphany, or of delusion? This
particular miracle of the returned psalter offers an image of
a book of poems (for that is what the psalms are, surpassed
in the Bible only by the Song of Songs) that is unchanged
by immersion. I shrink from the implication of an
immutable and scriptural authority for poetry: a canon that
is proof against the very processes of damp and dark decay
that Heaney has held on to earlier in the sequence, that
'other life that cleans our element'.

Far from returning to the green and muddy world of
growth as a symbol of wholeness and inspiration, the
pilgrim seems to have moved on into an abstract world,
that of the coded and immutable word. But he cannot,
surely, have gone over to all aspects of orthodoxy? The
epiphanies he offers seem cut off from everyday living,
almost wilfully remote: the mug not used for drinking but
for show, even at home; the lovers pledging themselves in
a fictional romance; the book of psalms that subsequently
became a handy symbol of God's authority for Ronan in his
territorial take-over bid.

And yet – the surface story is one of rejoicing and of
restorations. And the picture of a book of sacred poems
emerging from the deeps with its inks fast does offer a
much-needed emblem of salvage and survival after such
long-drawn-out grief and self-doubt.

My problem is to know which way to take the poem. I
cannot feel comfortable with its ambiguities of mood and
allegiance. I long for the moving waters, the bright green
cresses, of Sweeney's unreachable and pagan world. The

straightness of his flightlines tugs at my weary circling, the wildness of his haunts calls me from the visible hills that ring the lough. His absence from Heaney's text bothers me nearly as much as the absence of any image of lived love at 'the small hearths of constancy'.

NOTES

1. The strategies for producing a faint that are mentioned in this paragraph were solemnly believed in and practised at the author's convent boarding-school during the 1960s. Whether they worked through physical means or by auto-suggestion is open to question!
2. *An Image Darkly Forming*.
3. Nor Hall, *The Moon And The Virgin*, p.23.
4. The phrase is from another shaving poem, Thomas Kinsella's 'Mirror in February' (in *Downstream*), which draws interesting and possibly relevant parallels between the man shaving himself and Christ.
5. 'In Ireland, as throughout Atlantic Europe, the dresser ranks as the most important and elaborate piece of furniture in the kitchen ... In part of Ulster it is referred to as "the shelf".' E. Estyn Evans, *Irish Folk Ways*, p.91.
6. From 'Old Woman of the Roads', collected in *The Poet's Circuits*. And compare E. Estyn Evans, op. cit., p. 71· 'The open hearth with all its associations is truly the heart and centre of hearth and home. The fire is, with her children, the "care" of the woman of the house.'
7. *Faith Healer*, in *Selected Plays of Brian Friel*. And in real life, of course, Brian Friel and Stephen Rea founded Field Day, the Derry-based company that since 1980 has revived the tradition of nationwide tours of its productions. Heaney has been a member of Field Day's board since the early days.
8. Especially for a poet who is so devoted to driving! See Neil Corcoran again, *Seamus Heaney*, pp.64–67.

CHAPTER TWELVE

Although It Is the Night

Poem XI

3 August 1987: late morning and early afternoon
The day vigil

We make ... the discovery that we are irredeemably
alone in certain respects, and know that within the
territory of ourselves there can be only our footprints.

R.D. Laing, *The Divided Self*

A door in Toledo, detail

It is not until half-way through the second morning that I discover the fireplace in the women's hostel. Just inside the front door, in the corner of what looks like a school cloakroom, turves are smouldering on a grate-less hearth. A copper stands on a shelf above it, its gallons slowly heating from hand-warm to tongue-warm. I lean through the bodies huddled round the hearth to hold an earthenware mug – glazed simple white, with not a cornflower on it – to the copper's tap. This is 'Lough Derg soup': warmish water flavoured with a shake of salt and pepper. Then I retreat to the outer edges of the huddle and wait for my turn to be seated at the hearth's warmth. Gradually, as women leave restored, those of us standing on the margin win closer to the fire. At last a woman from the crowded bench gets up to go, and it is my turn to sit at the front and stretch my numb toes in the ashes.

We are pressed close, shoulder to shoulder. What talk there is is only of survival: getting to the end of *this* station, and memories and counts of stations survived in the past. There is none of the 'crack' of the Night Shelter. For all the women here are, like me, in their second day, sleepless, chilled and low in blood-sugar. The third-day pilgrims are away now to the mainland, and today's new pilgrims have not yet started to arrive.

Briefly, wistfully, we try to be indoor dwellers. But Lough Derg soup is about as close to proper soup as this hearth is to hearth and home. We are not even women here in any distinctive way, though we sit by the age-old symbol of woman's centring. There is no chat, no busyness: nothing to do.

And when we move after a few minutes' warmth to let another in, we walk out into the mixed crowd of women and men and away even from this meagre definition. Wandering about in the open, propping ourselves against walls for shelter and support, we are all – outwardly at – least well on the way to androgyny: swathed in woollies and macs, all equally unkempt and rumpled after yesterday's travelling and our sleepless night. There is no looking in the mirror for us yet-awhile.

It almost seems normal now to be thus: free of the usual mirror-definings of gender and status and family. Yes, there was that initial segregation of the sexes – men assigned to one hostel building to dump their things, women to the other, with the tiny width of the island between them. But the actual conduct of the pilgrimage makes no distinctions, and our *ad hoc* groupings and huddles through the long hours of this slack middle day are not dominated by gender, once we are away from the tiny fireplace each hostel has near its door. I think of all the old sepia photographs of the country people of Ireland: how the men are out and about in field and street, while the women are posed around the doorways of their homes. Here on the island we are all homeless, all workless. We are undefined by place or occupation, and also undefined – which is more startling perhaps for the women amongst us – by relationship.

And yet our physical and psychic dislocation from 'the world', and the sheer numbers of us who are in this together, combine to create an illusion of normality. This has become, in less than twenty-four hours, the only life we know. Unlike our lives off the island, so little is demanded of us. It is like being single again, and child-free. There is a certain luxury in this island life. I have found that I do not miss any of those I love. Is it that in my everyday life I too much miss my self?

In order, perhaps, to channel such introspection to devotional ends, brief diversions are scattered through the day: Renewal of Baptismal Promises at noon, Way of the Cross at three. And a second Lough Derg meal, of course, to be taken at some carefully chosen time – not too early or, with that one anticipation gone, time will drag even more. The 'kitchen' is open all day. It is not so much food that we have forsworn here, as meal-times, and all the rôles and demands and small ceremonies that go with them, and shape our days elsewhere.

All this time to fill – and yet there is only one set of the pilgrimage exercises, one basic station, to be made all day. Today's tougher circuit is not the circling of the stone beds. It is the hoop of boredom and lassitude that we pace or doze within.

I wander down to the small shop near the landing-stage, and fastidiously pick out a plain-covered pamphlet guide to Lough Derg from the showier paraphernalia of devotion. Several other pilgrims are in there, choosing framed photographs of the Pope, bottles for Lough Derg water, rosaries, holy pictures, pictures of the Sacred Heart. Outside Saint Mary's Church, I find a bench and start to read. There is a continual flow of pilgrims past me going to the appeal office in between shop and church. We have all been urged by the Prior at Morning Mass to contribute to the Lough Derg Building Fund.

One sentence in the guide takes me completely by surprise. A head-count of pilgrims in the late seventies showed that for every two men that came here, there were seven women. How extraordinary that, if it is still so, I had not observed such a striking difference for myself! For, of course, once it is pointed out I see the knots and gatherings of pilgrims with new eyes. Yes, less than ten years later the pattern still looks roughly the same. This, like most devotional habits in a Catholic country, is primarily a women's pilgrimage. And the huge new building that we are being urged to contribute to is the women's hostel. The old one is not just old: with the increase in the numbers of women pilgrims in the eighties, it's bursting at the seams.

I am astonished at my blindness to this imbalance between the sexes. Is it that men seem more numerous because they are more worthy of remark to me, a woman who grew up in women-only institutions but in a world where men are more 'important'? Or are the women less visible because I *expect* them to be the pious and devotional majority, as they are elsewhere in the churches of Ireland? And why are they in the majority? Are women in greater need of penance and prayer than men? Or is this an expression of their marginality within a patriarchal religion:

powerless, they need to sue to the Father with greater importunity?

I am cross with myself that my own gender has been invisible to me, as it is in so many ways in the world's reckoning, and crosser still with Heaney. He has sent his pilgrim self to this island that is so instinct at every level with the female, from the symbolism of its watery setting to the practice of the present-day faithful. He has raised many questions about the female within himself and within the process of writing; and within Catholicism and Ireland. And yet, in the poems he writes after waking from his night of Purgatory, the trail seems to be going dead, the discussion to be abruptly over. He cannot, surely, be going to leave the island without some awareness of the problems that he has summoned up along with his ghosts, without even a nod of recogntion?

And *I* am left here amongst a bunch of crazy, voluntary internees on a prison-rock circled by water! Suddenly I see this place as Michael and I saw it in January – an Irish Alcatraz. Then, I viewed it from afar. Now I am on it, and part of the pilgrim crowd that connives at penal servitude in some mass-delusion of criminal guilt.

And most of us are women.

I dream of spinning out from this shiftless circle at a tangent, of making a straight flight – as the crow flies, or a mad bird-king. But which direction would I take – west to the wild Atlantic and solitude? Or east to my own hearth?

*   *   *

It's getting worse. While I dream of flight, Heaney the pilgrim is homing in on obedience and faith. While I find dislocation and loss of identity, even of gender, on this Purgatory, he makes – as his very last act on the island – his confession to a man of the Church. The penance he is given is to translate the words of a canonised saint. The subject of the text is faith.

Poem X ended with a moment from *Buile Suibhne*; Poem XI begins with a second miracle of retrieval, an illumined and jewelled vision that makes me think of another early Christian text, the Anglo-Saxon *Dream of the Rood*. The pilgrim is still involved in childhood memories:

> As if the prisms of the kaleidoscope
> I plunged once in a butt of muddied water
> surfaced like a marvellous lightship
>
> and out of its silted crystals a monk's face
> that had spoken years ago from behind a grille
> spoke again about the need and chance
>
> to salvage everything, to re-envisage
> the zenith and glimpsed jewels of any gift
> mistakenly abased ...

The mandala of glowing colours made by the kaleidoscope's prisms rises up to the zenith like 'that sign covered with gold ... its crossbeam studded with jewels'.[1] The child's optical toy seems for a moment to take on the height and glory of a vision of the True Cross. Like the True Cross, which also was lost for years (until Helen, the mother of Constantine, discovered it), the kaleidoscope's glory had been obscured under mud. So this is miracle country again, the world of revelation. Like Ronan's psalter, the kaleidoscope is not subject to the laws of the natural world where things alter, and rot away. It seems that the pilgrim is moving still further towards contemplation of the abstract and symbolic moment. He is fixing his gaze on epiphanies now, rather than on the individuals who have peopled the main part of his Purgatory.

What of the poem within the poem, then, the specific poetic task set by the confessor as he sends the pilgrim on his way?

'Read poems as prayers,' he said, 'and for your
                                                  penance
translate me something by Juan de la Cruz.'

The choice, presumably, is up to the penitent. And he
chooses a poem that is an almost-abstract song of praise to
the Trinity, called 'The song of the soul that delights in
knowing God through faith.' Almost abstract, but not quite.
For through it flows the first *moving* water of this
pilgrimage, the living spring that is 'that fountain, filling,
running, / although it is the night.'

Although Heaney begins his own Poem XI with images
of light and zenith, this poem that he chooses to complete
it takes him down once more into darkness. He is in search
of salvage, and steadying: he finds in Juan's stanzas
unchartable and unplumbable deeps. It is as though he
needs to go back into the darkness before sunlight, the dark
beyond the 'dazzle of the impossible' (Poem X), in order to
know the 'haven and ... secrecy' (Poem XI) of the eternal
source.

'Through his poems and his prose works there run like
a refrain the words *secret, hidden, forgotten, in disguise,
silence, emptiness, night,*'[2] says Juan de la Cruz's biographer.
And the Spanish poet takes Heaney, himself a poet of both
articulated and unconscious absences, into the female
element of water, 'all sources' source and origin', and
together they begin a hymn of praise to its inexhaustible
and nourishing properties, its necessariness to all forms of
life, and its origins in the dark. At the liquid interplay of
vowels in its refrain, my heart lifts.

The theory of what *could* happen in this translation is,
for a moment, seductive. And yet the actualities of the text
finally have more to do with the theology of the all-male
Trinity[3] than with exploring the interconnections of human
love and nurture. Friends, lovers and colleagues are far
away. Even God, in Juan's text, seems unusually remote.
Poem and translation come across as a colloquy of the poet
and his own faith: it could be his inspiration too, but it's

hardly a muse. Despite its declared linking with the whole world of creatures and 'all peoples', its mood is solipsistic. Its imagery moves relentlessly towards the abstract. Again.

All the damp ditches and wells and rivers of Heaney's poetry could be part of this movement and mystery of the waters of the world, but while reading the words of his 'penance' I find it strangely difficult to bring them to mind. Lough Derg itself could reach down into its pre-Christian past, and its dark waters stir with the memory of the old religion's worship of water: basis of all life, chief means of healing and renewal . . . But this is a link that I have to make for myself. There is nothing in Heaney's translation to encourage it, or any links forged with his own 'personal Helicons'.[4] Heaney the penitent keeps to the straight rails of his chosen text, following its argument first to the allegory of the Trinity, and then to that of the bread of life. The ancient goddess he used to acknowledge, the female principle of life and birth, is potentially present in the material; Juan de la Cruz does not choose to articulate any of this (why should he?), but Heaney certainly does not go beyond his brief. How different from the trans-lating and jigsaw work with lines of Horace and Dante in his sixth poem . . .

By now the conduct of the Lough Derg pilgrimage seems very remote from Heaney's penance. Only the mantra-like repetition of each stanza'a refrain reminds me of the endless grind of the station prayers: 'although it is the night ... although it is the night ... although it is the night ...'. But I begin to resent the grudging air of that 'although', and wish Heaney had chosen some other poem of Juan de la Cruz, one with more welcome for the night. I think of what Frances Jaffer says about myth and its relationship to the male and female body:

> The Body, and its language, which is of course, all language. These notions of writing from the neck up ... But that male body, how IT dominates the culture, the environment, the language. Since 3,000BC in

Sumeria, Tiamat's monsters again and again, and
every myth an effort to keep the sun rising. Save the
sun, everybody, from the watery deeps, the dark
underneath it must go — Into — Every night into such
dangers, such soft inchoate darkness, what will
become of it, will it rise again? ... help the sun rise,
watch out for the dark underground, focus focus
focus, keep it high, let it soar, let it transcend, let it
aspire to Godhead ——[5]

In the context of the poems that have gone before, with
their persistently marginalised and silent female presences,
their passive men, and their images of a natural world
progressively contaminated and rendered powerless, the
choice of this particular poem for translation now fills me
with misgivings. To take over the waters of life with an
argument about the Trinity! Heaney's choice could, I
suppose, be seen as an inclusive and peacemaking gesture
of integration. But the fact that he has prefaced it with a
second image of light rising up miraculously from the dark
depths makes me worry that this is yet another move away
from the almost Taoist balance of his concluding remarks
to Carleton in Poem II, or the mowing images of Poem V.
There is no beginning of an answer, here or in the previous
poem, to his grim visions of passivity-in-action (so to
speak), of a community betrayed and betraying, of a source
and a terrain polluted with unlawful blood.

It is with the very word 'night' that he completes his
uneasy, unorthodox 'station'. Now, his penance accom-
plished, he is technically free to embark for the mainland.
But he leaves behind him a darkness impenetrable that I
would, somehow, wish to have as darkness visible.

There must have been, I suppose, a moment for his
departure. But that part of his boat journey back over the
lough's grey waters will be, like his entire boat journey
hither, unacknowledged in the writing.

*   *   *

I am still stuck firmly in the longueurs of the second day. There are several hours of daylight to go, and a night on an iron bedstead at the end of them. I begin to walk and count my way round my sole station of this middle day, and by the time I have reached the beds of Saint Brigid and Saint Brendan it is raining steadily. The knees of my jeans are soaked through as soon as I kneel on the puddled walls and flagstones. There is no shortage *here* of mud or silt or running water.

By the time I have circled my way down to the water's edge, the rain has blown away, and the meagre sun of a Donegal August has coaxed a hatch of caddis flies from the lough waters. They cluster and spin in the air over the thin reeds and Saint Patrick's kneeling-stones. So many new and alive creatures! They are small and sooty-black, and when one of them lands on my hand I see that it folds its wings at the back like the bevelled head of a horseshoe nail. Its antennae are like the dark fronds of dendrites laid down in seams of coal.

Sooty and born of mud from the lake's bottom, they console me for what I see as Heaney's defection from the world of damp and dung. As the sun strengthens and my jeans stiffen into semi-dryness, I think myself back, too, to the warmth and delight and harvest of the sixth poem: 'Freckle-face, fox-head, pod of the broom ...' In it the words of Horace and Dante brought Italy and the south for brief moments to the cold northern stones of Saint Patrick's Purgatory, breathed the welcome air of another country, other centuries, on to a station that has been so relentlessly and narrowly Irish.

If he has now brought an air of 'Spain to our chapped wilderness', I do not want to dismiss it lightly. And a poem from sixteenth century Spain has entered the text *complete*: not just a fragment of quotation this time. Once again Heaney has taken the trouble to give one of his rare notes of attribution at the back of the book. It's only the name of Juan's poem, but again I want to explore the named text's hinterland, to discover whether it offers, like the snippets of Horace and Dante, reconciliations and illuminations not apparent in Heaney's translation of its words.

I sit with my back to the hostel wall on stone flags still damp from the rain. Heaney's sequence has, after all, landed me in this comfortless spot. Now I shall take the excuse of his hint, and travel – in spirit at least – to Spain. I open Gerald Brenan's *Life of John of the Cross*. It is just what I need to pass this long afternoon, and it looks suitably devotional to nearby pilgrims who sneak a look at the title, or ask me what I'm reading. 'Read poems as prayers, read prayers as poems ...' I want to discover why and when the original poem was written.

1578. It is the morning of the feast of the Assumption of the Virgin, the fifteenth day of a hot and humid August. In all the churches and convents of Toledo, the angelus bells are ringing out for the feast day. A man is hurrying through the streets, his clothes torn and matted, his thin shoulders covered in weals and sores. He knocks urgently at the grille of a convent of enclosed Carmelite nuns, and, amazingly, all three sets of doors are quickly unlocked and then locked again behind him. He, a man, is allowed into the order's strict enclosure.

The nuns are heavily veiled in black muslin. It hangs down over the white of their habits. They are gathering round this emaciated man, offering him a dish of pears stewed in cinnamon, listening anxiously and with growing delight to his story. When two clean and well-fed friars come hotfoot to the grille at the street door with constables, seeking Juan, they are sent away – no men, they are firmly told, may enter the enclosure! Within, Juan de la Cruz is standing, holding on to the chapel grille in his exhaustion, and reciting urgently, to the nuns in the choir beyond, the verses of his *Cantico espiritual*, and then the poem that begins

> *Que bien se yo la fonte que mana y corre ...*
> How well I know that fountain, filling, running ...

He is so thin and disfigured from hunger that, as one of them later said, 'he looked like an image of death'.[6] Last night, he tells them, he made a classic escape from his enemies, the 'unreformed' party within the disputing factions of the Carmelite Order. He slid down a rope of torn blanket strips on to the coping of Toledo's city walls, within a couple of feet of the drop to the gorge of the Tagus river, and then jumped into the street.

He has been held captive for eight months in conditions close to those of Saint Patrick's Purgatory: in hunger and in darkness. What he has lacked of its experience has been the companionship of its community – and its fresh air. His confinement has been solitary. But he *has* had the river. Outside, directly beneath his useless slit window, the Tagus runs in its rocky bed. Throughout the winter and the spring, he has heard the river's changes of note and volume: the great rumble of the snow-melt, the shorter-lived spates of the late spring rains, its slackening to sluggish summer.

In the hot weather recently, while the river was quieter, he says that another sound reached him, a snatch of a love song from the street outside:

> *Muerome de amores,*
> *Carillo. Que hare?*
> *– Que te mueras, alahe.*

> I am dying of love, beloved.
> What shall I do?
> – Die.

He suddenly saw how he might turn such popular song lyrics 'a lo divino'.

The song of the eternal fountain was probably one of the first of the poems Juan de la Cruz had written during that dark and echoing captivity. The water imagery in it is right for Station Island, even though the waters that girdle it are still; and the prison cell where it was composed goes with the dark time before returning to light and freedom. All the circle images of Heaney's sequence – the small, land-locked circuits of the saints' beds, the limiting circuits of custom and the worn ones of grief, the tramped-down grass of promise – are taken up in the vast and essential rain-cycle of the Spanish poem.

And yet, Juan de la Cruz's 'Dark Night' has a specific mystical significance that seems to sort ill with its appearance at this place in Heaney's sequence. 'By the darkness of night is meant the darkness of faith, which ... leads and guides the soul on its journey.' During its journey the spirit is gradually purged of every attachment to the created world and its creatures, 'until it reaches the ineffable moment when it is transformed into its Lover – *amada en el Amado.*'[7] This movement towards a mystical purgation, an emptying of self, has not been what has concerned Heaney's pilgrimage at all. His late twentieth century angst has been highly individualised, and tied down to places and times and persons. He is a fine poet, but not, I think, a mystic. And by lifting this poem of Juan's out of its philosophical matrix, and letting it down unchanged into his own mess of unresolved personal and historical questions, he has further confused me.[8]

And has left me with yet another absence to lament: that mystic union of *'amada en el Amado'* that is understood, but not directly represented, in this particular poem of Juan de la Cruz. In so many of his other lyrics, it is joyously bodied forth in words that carry on the mystical-erotic tradition of the *Song of Songs*. Not so here, but Brenan does find strong echoes of a famous Galician romance at the heart of the poem, in the use of the form *fonte* instead of the expected Castilian *fuente*: the reference is to a magic spring which offers consolation and even ecstasy to troubled lovers.[9] Not a trace of this vital element in Juan's work is translated into Heaney's dutiful penance.

I have followed the trail. Would that I could take it to

Toledo in body as well as in mind! As I close Brenan's book and walk down to the edge of the water, I feel even more unsatisfied with the omissions and assumptions in Heaney's solitary 'sacrament of reconciliation', more than ever restless and impatient with my own confinement.

NOTES

1. Freely translated from *The Dream of the Rood* edited by Bruce Dickins and Alan S.C. Ross, lines 6-9.
2. Gerald Brenan, *St John of the Cross*, p.84.
3. The Father, Son and Holy Ghost. Although it could be argued that the Holy Spirit is not necessarily masculine, it is usually referred to with masculine epithets and phraseology.
4. See Chapter 7 above.
5. Frances Jaffer was a contributor to the workshop essay 'For the Etruscans: Sexual Difference and Artistic Production – The Debate over a Female Aesthetic' by Rachel Blau DuPlessis and Members of Workshop 9 in *The Future of Difference* edited by Hester Eisenstein and Alice Jardine.
6. Brenan, op. cit., p.37.
7. Ibid., p.125.
8. T.S. Eliot takes part of Juan's verses on the *via negativa* (*Ascent of Mount Carmel* I, 13) into 'East Coker III': another version of a twentieth century descent into the Underworld, and one which is entirely peopled by male figures! Although Eliot and Heaney are writing from very different starting points, their use of Juan's words leaves a similar impression of dislocation from the sources of life and nourishment.
9. *Fonte frida y con amor*, the Galician romance that he alludes to in his commentary on his own *Cantico Espiritual*. See Brenan, op. cit., pp.113-115.

PART THREE

Off the Island

CHAPTER THIRTEEN

His Straight Walk

Poem XII

Tuesday 4 August 1987: morning
The final 'station'

Blinding in Paris, for his party-piece
Joyce named the shops along O'Connell Street
And on Iona Colmcille sought ease
By wearing Irish mould next to his feet.

Seamus Heaney, 'Gravities'

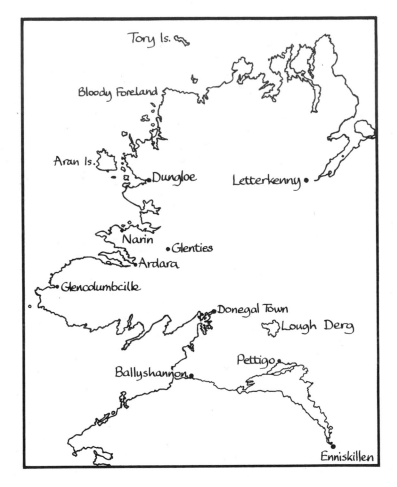

Co. Donegal

The single night's sleep in my curtained cubicle is squeezed from my humming head like a pip: one moment it is ten at night, and I'm pulling the stiff linen sheet up round my neck; the next it is six in the morning and the waking bell is ringing. I've had no dreams at all that I can remember – and I'm not one bit refreshed.

Morning Mass is grim. I am hemmed in by swaying and semi-conscious survivors of last night's vigil, and feel cut off from the now-familiar faces of my own day's pilgrims. There seem to be strangers all around me. It's that recurring wish to belong – I cannot shake it off. But when 'our' turn comes for the Papal Blessing that we have earned by completing our station, I set my teeth against it, and lurk gratefully amongst the second-dayers. Hundreds of women – and I see now more clearly than yesterday that it *is* mainly women – hold up rosaries and other devotional talismans to receive this special favour. They are duly dipped and glamoured . . .

'Papal Blesing' – the words bring to mind the flushed face of one of my Galway cousins when he heard some good news: 'This calls for a papal blessing, wouldn't you say?' he grinned, and took a bottle of Jameson's out of the cupboard behind him. I realise how starved I am of the irreverent and playful side of Irish talk. There is little irony, little bite, in the sweetness of Station Island. I smile to myself in anticipation, catch my neighbour's puzzled eye, and try to make the grin more pious-looking. Still dissembling. Oh, how tired I am of this!

Outside once more to do my ninth and last station, I rattle round the basilica and beds, an expert at my rigmarole of counting – but by this stage prayers or numbers would be equally mantra-like. I half-regret the subterfuge now. Would I have won through to some stronger feeling of kinship with the past and with this place, would I at last be planting my still-bare feet on speaking stones, if I had not reneged on that one matter of the prayers? But I don't want to be a believer again, do I? Not in the Catholic fold, certainly; but there are the elder faiths, with their spirits of stone and water that I had thought to find here. Both in my own Station and in Heaney's sequence they have eluded me.

Too late. Time presses. Now all I want to do is to get clear of this place, and to look elsewhere for any affirmations that Ireland can still offer me. And I can start by stripping my one-night bed. We have been asked to do this, and to make up our beds with fresh linen for the next batch of pilgrims, who will soon begin to arrive. There is no time even to linger at the water's edge. I wash my ingrained feet at one of the low sinks on the ground floor of the women's hostel, and hurry up the stairs to my task. The clean sheets take the sharp creases of their hospital corners like card. I gather my few things into the rucksack, and put on my shoes again.

Suddenly it feels like the last day of term at my convent boarding-school, that unreachable morning that would never ever come. Then the final date on the hand-drawn calendar would be crossed out at last – with lipstick, of course (did the nuns ever guess it was that?) – and we'd take out our folded and almost forgotten 'own clothes' from the bottom of the drawer. After less than forty-eight hours' absence, my socks and shoes feel as strange to my feet as those clothes did then to my uniformed self. But, as with them, only for a moment. They take my warmth and my shape to heart in the time it takes to walk to the dormitory door.

I dance down the long flights of stairs, and right past the statue of Our Lady. I'm at the bottom before I remember that I have something to return to her. So I leave my bag in the hall and slip back up to the landing. Good. No one else is coming down. It only takes a moment to drape the blue glass rosary over the statue's pressed-together praying hands.

'I'm leaving,' I tell the sweet face, 'and for good. It's not enough, you know, just making statues like this one move down in Co. Cork – bits of plaster. Or putting on appar-itions over in Yugoslavia. We don't need you as miracle or as 'glamour'. We need an image of woman that's as basic and essential as – water.' Heaney's poem has at least given me this.

But the image I have of water at this moment is a sudden, unbidden memory from Cavan town, where the bus stopped for a change of driver on the way up to Lough Derg. I leant over a bridge and saw a river whitened and frothy with effluent from belching drains along its banks. It cut its course through a bed of junked metals.

And I look again at Our Lady, and think of two recent images of motherhood that have shaken Ireland quite as much as news of the moving statues. Of fifteen-year-old Ann Lovett dying alone in childbirth, with her baby, at the Lourdes grotto in the small town of Granard – and of the appalling small-town silence that followed her death.[1] Of the Kerry Babies Tribunal, and all the bizarre and degrading insinuations it made against the unmarried mother Joanne Hayes, who was not technically on trial at all And the all male body of men that stood in judgement: 'What have I got to do with the women of Ireland in general? What have the women of Ireland in general got to do with this case?' asked the judge as it drew to a close.[2]

But the case is not simple. Mary offers *me* no usable image of womanhood, and yet for these two mothers and for the thousands of Irish women and men who gave them and their families the support of prayers and letters, it was Mary the Mother of God, Mother of Mercy, who offered a direct line of intercession to a God of compassion as well as of justice. They could appeal to her over the heads of the human and patriarchal authorities who were studiously turning away, or judging them. Mary can offer, then, strange but practical ways of apparently bypassing the male-dominated power-structures. She's like Eve whom she's supposed to supersede, Eve who made the *felix culpa* or 'lucky mistake' of eating the apple in Eden. And I remember the prayer of my childhood that quickened all communal devotions to Mary with a great urgency of love and hope: 'Hail, Holy Queen, Mother of Mercy, hail our

life, our sweetness and our hope. To Thee do we come,
poor banished children of Eve ...'

*   *   *

It is a bittersweet leave-taking. I know that I shall not come
to this island ever again. As I walk in new foot-comfort
along its wide paths, taking a 'last look' at the basilica, the
stone circles, the mound, Saint Mary's Church, I feel that I
am leaving behind not just the faith of my childhood, but
the assumptions of much of the first half of my life. I
thought, in 1968, that I could give up that faith with a clean
break, and leave it all behind me. Not until I came to
Station Island on this supposedly literary quest did I realise
how much the afterlife of that faith's habits has haunted my
post-catholic living.

Shall I ever be clear of its 'offer it up' reflexes? As a
mother I feel reasonably sure of growing out of them. What
I have loved about parenting has been the constant tug
between my slower and adult metabolic rate (in all
respects) and my children's vivid rate of spurts and
plateaux. Every year, every day, they have shown me how
to be a mother, and the perk of the job has been that I have
also learnt from it, gradually, how to be myself. It is as a
lover and a partner that I feel I have far more to learn.
Before men I do not, I hope, bow down, but I have an
alarming tendency to 'offer up', to postpone my own needs
– with no prospect, as with children, that time will relieve
me progressively of the sacrifice. I will return to Michael
with new and sobering thoughts for our never-completed
discussion: how to live in mutual and balancing egality,
when we both grew up in a world without feminist
perspectives. But a chilly sense that there are areas here
that are beyond articulation, out of reach of discussion,
nags at the corner of my thoughts about Michael and me.
Is habit's afterlife like radiation's, a series of half-lives over

spans of years? An afterlife that will never, in my lifetime, become insignificant in its ill effects?

I cannot tell whether being on the island is giving me a new objectivity, or sending me wildly wrong. But at least I shall have a few days out of all this before I must go home . . .

Here on the island there have been other, slight relationships. As I walk to the landing-stage, my thoughts return from home and I look out for the individuals with whom I've shared a word, even a smile, on the pilgrimage: the woman I steadied as she threw up the pure water of exhaustion in the small hours of the night vigil; my bus companions; those with whom I broke the hard oatcakes of Lough Derg; those with whom I talked at greater length. Now even the pilgrims of my own day seem unfamiliar. Can their shod feet, and a change of clothing here and there, have changed them so? I cannot even see Thérèse and her friends in the crowd. I wonder what thoughts Billy has now about the pilgrimage. Is he still in a dangerous state of doubt? I saw Thérèse carefully steer him clear of me a couple of times yesterday, suspicious, perhaps, of that inability of mine to say the Hail Mary behind the basilica during the Night Vigil.

Two enormous open boats have arrived to take us to the shore. We're told that over a hundred and fifty will fit into the bigger one, and in a few moments the prior himself has handed me into it. As the boat leaves the landing-stage, he starts us off singing 'Hail Glorious Saint Patrick / Dear saint of our isle,' the vigorous Saint Patrick's Day hymn that I haven't heard for twenty years. The rising sixth of its opening phrase is truly glorious, but as soon as we are clear of the island, the singing thins and dies away, hardly half-way through the first verse. Are we all becoming separate, self-conscious, already remembering that we are people with other identities than that of pilgrim?

The community of the island is being dismantled, and now our 'real' communities will begin to reclaim us. For me there are a few days left in which I can be undefined, can do my Sweeney act the length and breadth of Donegal. I wonder for how many of my companions Station Island is the one destination, this community the one solitude, the travelling hither and home again the one journey from the hearth that they are permitted – or permit themselves. The Station is sanctioned by custom, and sanctified by its structures of sacrament and penitence. Do they not thirst, as I do, for the real solitude of the open road? How rare it is for women in this country, in any country, to have even Station Island's circumscribed freedom in order to become their unencumbered selves for three days.

I remember a dream I used to have at the time I was starting to write poetry again after years of silence. A party of women are walking in single file and in silence. Stone-age or iron-age women. They leave their encampments behind them, their pots simmering on slow fires, and walk from the mid-lands of habitation to the edges of the ocean. There they stand on high cliffs gazing out at its vastness, leaning on its winds. Burnished and translucent in the salt air, they turn reluctantly at last for home. In their absence, the men have been making charcoal-clamps and soot-houses. The women find the encampment dark with smoke, and their hearths white with ash. The pots are still warm. They have not boiled dry, or burned. The women have hardly been away – in the men's measurable time.

Our crossing back seems to take no time at all either. The boat slides alongside the jetty and I step up and across the gunwale on to its concrete. Cars are revving up already in the car-park. Buses are banked at the top of the rise. One of them should take me to Enniskillen.

*   *   *

Like a convalescent, I took the hand
stretched down from the jetty ...

Sometime in the early years of the eighteenth century, the blind harpist O'Carolan took hold of a hand stretched down to him at this self-same moment of arrival at the ferry-house quay.

'By the hand of my godfather, this is the hand of Brigid Cruise!' he cried, recognising the touch of his first love, the girl he'd written songs and tunes for in his distant youth, before the smallpox blinded him at the age of eighteen. It's a romantic story, and one still related fondly at Lough Derg.

> Then I knew him in the flesh
> out there on the tarmac among the cars, ...

The hand that is held out to Heaney is 'fish-cold and bony', and male: it is the helping hand of James Joyce. Although he is as dead as any other speaking ghost of this pilgrimage, he is the only one of them that is not caught in contraries, or some distress. He is also the only one of whom the pilgrim Heaney says 'I knew him in the flesh'. The phrase is startling. It has two Old Testament echoes that I find difficult to put out of mind: Job's intimation of the body's immortality, 'I know that in my flesh I shall see God'; and the specialised sense of 'carnal knowledge'. Is Joyce going to offer Heaney some strange spiritual consummation, some new knowing 'between chaps',[3] in order to bring this troubled sequence to a conclusion?

Not only does Joyce make a first physical contact with the pilgrim, but he moves the agenda further away than ever from the green and rural world. This final, confirming ghost is a creature of the city, at home with tarmac and cars and litter baskets. His message is the artist's necessary dissociation from society, his 'outsider' position; but his images of artistic activity are very different from King Sweeney's distressed and random flittings, his recalcitrant and externally imposed exile.

Everything Joyce tells Heaney is about acting alone, and taking the initiative. He offers the distinctively masculine

'quest' as a pattern for the poet's life-long journey;
pilgrimage seems passé as a metaphor for it now, the idea
of repeating circles on one spot seems a 'common rite'.

> 'Your obligation
> is not discharged by any common rite.
> What you must do must be done on your own ...
>
> Let go, let fly, forget.
> You've listened long enough. Now strike your note ...
>
> Keep at a tangent.
> When they make the circle wide, it's time to swim
>
> out on your own ...'

But what does he say in 1984 that has not already been said
in essence to the poet by the novelist Michael MacLaverty
twenty-two years earlier?

> Royal
> Avenue, Belfast, 1962,
> A Saturday afternoon, glad to meet
> Me, newly cubbed in language, he gripped
> My elbow. 'Listen. Go your own way.
> Do your own work.'[4]

Joyce does have something to add to that admonition: the
rubbishing of the 'peasant pilgrimage' that Heaney the
pilgrim has been trying, though with minimal success, to
make for the last nine poems. Even Heaney's personal
delight at a link between his own birthday and a turning-
point in Stephen Dedalus's discovery of the difference
between English and Irish-English in *Portrait of the Artist* is
brushed aside.[5]

> 'Who cares,'
> he jeered, 'any more? The English language

> belongs to us ...
> That subject people stuff is a cod's game ...'

And yet the whole of the 'Station Island' sequence has been painfully documenting and revolving just that 'subject people stuff'. For the Catholics of the Six Counties it is by no means a dead issue. For over sixty years, they have seen themselves as the Irish remnant still held in the colonial state that the twenty-six counties have shaken off. And it is this very confronting of what it means to be 'subject people' that has made the sequence so concerned with the damaged and damaging aspects of the feminine, the 'shadow-feminising' of a whole section of the population.

Joyce, whose Molly Bloom never stirs from the supine during the whole of *Ulysses*, hardly seems the person to bring a resolution here. His voice may, in Heaney's opinion, 'edd[y] with the vowels of rivers', but the advice he utters in it is robustly and inconsiderately masculine. He has nothing to say to the feminine side of Heaney's would-be androgynous muse. He tells him to be active and solitary, to 'write / for the joy of it. Cultivate a work-lust.' And that 'work-lust' operates in a most curious and solely masculine way, in images both physical and abstract:

> ... a work-lust
> that imagines its haven like your hands at night
>
> dreaming the sun in the sunspot of a breast.

How remote now this tarmac conversation seems from the earlier one with William Carleton about 'earthworms of the earth' and 'another life that cleans our element'. And, as an ending, how far from the final stanzas of the *Commedia*, where Dante felt himself to be on the edge of something more powerful than his own words could express, a single impulse of love that bound together the original act of creation and all human love and justice, 'the love that moves the sun and other stars'.

For Heaney here and for Heaney's Joyce – can their voices be usefully distinguished? – the act of writing and the idiosyncracy of 'voice' seem all-important. No mention is made of the what or the why of this writing; the how is the thing.

> Keep at a tangent.
> When they make the circle wide, it's time to swim
>
> out on your own and fill the element
> with signatures on your own frequency,
> echo soundings, searches, probes, allurements,
>
> elver-gleams in the dark of the whole sea.

The quondam somnambulist, who listened out for encounters between 'masculine will and intelligence and feminine clusters of image and emotion',[6] is urged by the ghost of Joyce to become a sort of Captain Nemo of the deeps: questing, invasive, egotistical. How different this sea-life is from the older traditions of oarless *peregrinatio* in a skin boat! In giving Joyce these tough lines to speak, and apparently attending to them, Heaney seems to be reneging on a key early fosterer, the Wordsworth who gave him the concept of 'a wise passiveness, a surrender to energies that spring within the centre of the mind.'[7]

Heaney leaves Purgatory thus, with Joyce's 'quick and clean' masculine voice in his ears. On the island he has been 'down among the women', back in the world that is 'centred towards a feminine presence.' He has tried one more time the path of humility and of bowing down, the 'lived thing of prayers', and the patience that he once said was 'probably ... the best virtue'.[8]

'There's a kind of voice in the world that's deprived because it hasn't got something feminine in it or about it,' he went on, in that conversation recorded in the period between *North* and *Fieldwork*. 'It's just a conviction I have that some kind of wholeness, of content, is a good thing

and is possible.'[9] Does that possibility no longer hold for
him, now that he has seen aspects of the feminine become
so identified with the difficulties of his people? And blamed
in some way for his troubled sense of wrong turnings in his
own poetic vocation?

Opposite the last few lines of the last poem in 'Station
Island', 'SWEENEY REDIVIVUS' is printed in capitals. It is the
third part of the *Station Island* collection. I cannot quite
believe in that suggested restoration to life; or if I must, I
feel Sweeney's resurrection will be for me like Lazarus's,
swaddled with winding cloths, hampered and reluctant.

*   *   *

I have never before walked so closely, and barefoot, in the
Wenceslas steps of a poet. Were I to dress in white, and live
for a season in that upstairs room in Amherst, would my
reading of Emily Dickinson's poems be so radically altered?
Walking the words of Heaney's sequence, I have found that
my reading of its last three poems has altered profoundly.
I am reluctant now to read on into the poems of 'Sweeney
Redivivus', which up to now has been my favourite section
of the whole collection.

I sit on the Enniskillen bus and, in the stillness before
departure, hunt out the notebook I filled before leaving
home. I reread the notes I made, only weeks and days
before, about those last three poems. I do not find there the
confusion and disappointment that I feel now. I thought
then: how generous of Heaney to include the choleric
Ronan, how lovely that he translates a lyric from the
imprisonment of Juan de la Cruz, how bracing that he
meets Joyce when he steps on to the mainland shore. But
living the pilgrimage, however inadequately and
idiosyncratically, has altered my reading of the texts. The
unstated and the unresolved now hammer their absences
home.

I do not want this change.

I came here because, at home and in England, I could not understand why the sequence, with its male speakers and surface male concerns, gave me so strong a sense of the feminine. Having stalked the poems' elusive women, and heard the male ghosts' words spoken in this place of powerlessness and supplication, I now understand more about the disabling links between feminine and masculine in Irish Catholic culture, in Heaney's work – and, a little, in myself. But following in the footsteps of the waking, third-day Heaney has brought me no illumination. The problem of this communal, even national, disablement seems to have been raised, tentatively at first, then more centrally as the men begin to bear witness; and it is shown at last *in extremis* in the death of the hunger-striker. After that it is ignored, or strangely side-stepped.

It is, of course, naive and unhistorical to expect a Dantean resolution. That all-embracing spiritual and political cosmos powered by God's love has long since fragmented beyond even a poet's making-good. But if 'the god has, as they say, withdrawn', is that not all the more reason for drawing on all that is human in us? For not narrowing down the range to such a partial and masculine way of looking, after the complex and troubled wide-angle of the first nine poems? Those poems took me into difficult and forgotten areas, suggested disturbing and illuminating connections in both the individual and communal life of my native country. Took me into, and out of, myself. For that distressing illumination I am indeed grateful. In the poems that close the sequence, though, I sense a withdrawal by Heaney from the painful and complex areas of the feminine that he has uncovered during his 'otherworldly' spell.

In doing the station of Saint Patrick's Purgatory, Heaney and I have not just revisited the beliefs and practices of Catholic Ireland. On this stone island set in the midst of the waters, we have been through a ceremony of death and rebirth with ancient roots that predate and nourish its Christian existence. We have participated in a particular and physical enaction of myth, such as is rare in the modern world, though its symbolic meaning is universal and alive.

It is a myth, however, that is still seen in overwhelmingly masculine terms. Little seems to have changed since Conan, in the old naming story, was ingested by the female monster, and birthed himself by cutting an exit through her belly.[10] I think wryly of Tom Phillips' notes to his illuminated version of Dante's *Inferno*. He says of the bushes and breast in his frontispiece's imagery:

> ... any visit to the underworld is a rape of Mother Earth, whose hairy entranceway within this landscape is the *Selva Oscura* (cf. Canto 1/1). Also present, and rising out of the sea, is the Mountain of Purgatory, forming as it were an ancillary breast to the rocky reclining figure, Purgatory being the place of spiritual nurture.[11]

Heaney's experience of Station Island is a fragmented and reluctant part of this long male-oriented tradition; not a rape – there is no implication of violence or forcing in Heaney's pilgrim persona, rather the reverse – but certainly an entering of the female realm that is intimate, in darkness, with the cycle of growth and death. But in taking on this mythic material, he has not offered, at least to me, a usable rewriting of it, or even a questioning of it, such as I have grown to expect from his work. Although his entering in is tender and tentative, his emergence into the upper world is hard-edged and final. He leaves on the straight course of a tangent, heading out to sea and on his own, on a paradigm of the classic male 'quest' journey. He is told (tells himself?) that his 'work' henceforward is to be a high-profile and high-technology trawling of the deeps.

For the woman artist, or hero(ine), or pilgrim on the same life's road, what does the male version of the journey to the underworld offer? She, too, must re-enter the world of darkness and then re-emerge from it into the world of light. But whereas the male hero is assumed to be reborn once and for all, she returns and returns into the fructifying, inchoate source. For her, Persephone with her seasonal returns is the archetype, not Orpheus, and even less someone like Aeneas, founder of Rome's patriarchy and imperium, who made the classic underworld journey that so many subsequent ones are modelled on.

> Poor men with their linear time stretching away into an infinity that defeats the imagination. They don't understand that it all goes round and round, going away and coming back like the moon.[12]

Although I feel the tug of the tangent, I am part of the world of circles and circuits, of Persephone's cyclical travel between over- and underworld, her constant retreading of the path from day to dark and from dark to day. And it has been the Persephone in Heaney that I have loved and listened out for over the years, his constant re-opening of that 'door into the dark'. And listened out, too, for the Orpheus in him, turned humble and persistent, trying again and again to coax and understand a Eurydice reluctant, like Rilke's,[13] to become a full-time denizen once again of the upper world of light.

I have often felt uneasy about the representation of women in Heaney's work – the women of *North* in particular – but I have also felt that there was a transparency and a serious intent about his listening out for the female in himself that made him a rare writer, and a rare man, in Ireland. But his pilgrim self's hasty and unresolved departure from the Purgatory has left *me* behind, worrying about all he has not dealt with.

The woman of 'Station Island's' sixth poem will never, now, turn round and show her face. The moment has passed her by. The wheatlands of her back remain fixed in an outworn image of agrarian fertility. There's no helping hand to bring her to the city, or even 'the whole sea'; to the present day in Ulster, or to the world that most of us live in. And the speaking souls of the dead men, caught still in the bitter moments of their dying, do not even have the traditional consolation of Purgatory – that through self-knowledge, and the prayers of the living, they will work their way to eventual bliss and an understanding of their lives' part in humanity's larger picture. They are left behind, with no contemporary equivalent to Dante's *tre donne gentile* to watch over them; nor any corresponding masculine spirit(s) to restore to them that essential faith in this post-Christian era – faith in themselves.

I look back at this remote outpost of Purgatory through the window of the Enniskillen bus. The Island itself returns to the scale it had when I first saw it from this same car-park last January. Across the grey waters it has shrunk again to that huddle of buildings so closely packed that my January eye could not imagine the open spaces, the lawns, the slope down to the water's edge. The white of the new women's hostel and the verdigris of the basilica's dome pucker together, draw in to conceal the hundreds of pilgrims at the island's heart.

Today's arrivals are already queuing at the ferryhouse.

NOTES

1. See 'The Death of Ann Lovett' in *The Best of Nell* by Nell McCafferty. Ann Lovett died on 31 January 1984.
2. Quoted in *A Woman to Blame* by Nell McCafferty, p.169. The Tribunal sat from 28 December 1984 to June 1985.
3. Compare 'I think that the "Hail Mary" is more of a poem than the "Our Father". "Our Father" is between chaps, but there's something faintly amorous about the "Hail Mary"'.' John Haffenden, *Poets in Conversation*, p.61.
4. 'Fosterage', in *North*.
5. '... there is a moment in Stephen's diary
   for April the thirteenth, a revelation

   set among the stars – that one entry
   has been a sort of password in my ears,

the collect of a new epiphany,

the Feast of the Holy Tundish.' ...

April the thirteenth is Heaney's own birthday. See Chapter V of
Portrait of the Artist as a Young Man. The (English) dean of studies
has just demonstrated to Stephen Dedalus that he has mastered
one of 'the useful arts' that we have in addition to 'the liberal
arts': he has lit a fire in the large grate of a lecture theatre.
Standing by the hearth(!), the two men discuss aesthetics, and the
dean gives the example of Epictetus and his lamp. The liberal and
the useful arts meet for a moment:

> - To return to the lamp, he said, the feeding of it is also a
> nice problem. You must choose the pure oil and you must
> be careful when you pour it in not to overflow it, not to
> pour in more than the funnel can hold.
> - What funnel? asked Stephen.
> - The funnel through which you pour the oil into your
> lamp.
> - That? said Stephen. Is that called a funnel? Is it not a
> tundish?
> - What is a tundish?
> - That. The . . . funnel.
> - Is that called a tundish in Ireland? asked the dean. I never
> heard the word in my life.
> - It is called a tundish in Lower Drumcondra, said Stephen,
> laughing, where they speak the best English.

See Neil Corcoran, *Seamus Heaney*, pp.167/8, for further
discussion of this reference.

6.   *Preoccupations*, p.34.
7.   Ibid., p.63.
8.   Haffenden, op.cit., p.60.
9.   Ibid., p.61.
10.   See Chapter Two above.
11.   *Dante's Inferno*, p.284.
12.   Gillian Allnutt, *Spitting the Pips Out*, p.116.
13.   See 'Orpheus. Eurydice. Hermes.' in *Rilke Selected Poems*
translated by J.B. Leishman (Penguin Books, 1964), a selection
made from the Hogarth Press edition of 1960.

CHAPTER FOURTEEN

On the Road

4–7 August 1987:
Boa Island, west Donegal, and home

I give you this, my opened map of flight.

Carol Rumens, 'The Most Difficult Door'

The Caldragh Idol, Boa Island

4 August

Pettigo.

The stalls are out, laden with the daintiest water biscuits, the finest oatcakes. The buses stop for a quarter of an hour while we stock up. Today we will each of us make our own private 'Lough Derg meal', and the dry bread of it can be anything from soft fresh baps to designer crispbread. And we can drink as many minerals[1] as we like, whenever we like.

Under the Border bridge the Termon River flows on to Lough Erne unregarded. The back walls of the town's warehouses and stores that stand sheer on its banks are windowless. Underwater gleams from old prams and rusty cookers are the coins in this fountain, and effluents from open drains are its latterday libations. But there are beds of wild watercresses too, and though I do not see the mad king Sweeney stooping from the sky to their bright green trails, moorhen and grey wagtail are busy on their fringes. A water ousel's white front flashes as it flies with quick wingbeats downstream.

*   *   *

Enniskillen.

I have managed, with great difficulty and much footslogging, to find a garage in Enniskillen that will 'loan' me a car for the two days I have free. It is far too close to the Border and the Trouble, they tell me, for regular car-hire firms to operate in the town any more. 'You'd need to know who you'd be hiring it to,' the garage owner says, looking me up and down thoughtfully. At last he relents, but I have to fix up all the insurance with my own firm in England. During one of the long phonecalls he realises that I'm checking on cover to go into the Republic. 'What on earth would you want to go *there* for?' he hisses, and I worry that he's going to refuse me the car. I say something about archaeological sites that seems to settle him. It is difficult to remember that the Border is only twelve miles away to the west.

I don't, of course, say that I've just come from Lough Derg. I've known all along – in the way one does here – that he is a Protestant, but he doesn't guess that I'm a Catholic. My English accent has put him right off the scent.

*   *   *

Boa Island again.

'It'll say Caldragh Cemetery, the signpost you're after,' the man in Enniskillen's Tourist Information office says at last, after much poring over large-scale maps. There are big display photographs of the famous stone heads behind his desk. Telling me how to track down the heads themselves is not so straightforward. 'But it'll likely be only a wee bit of a wooden one. Take the A47 over the island, and keep your eyes peeled.'

And now I am walking down a farm track on Boa, eyeing the red detail of high summer. Herb robert leaves. The stems of the meadowsweet. Scarlet and bronze of the oak's second flush of growth. Ragged robin in the reedy meadow. Wild strawberries' red runners and edge-leaves, and redder fruits.

And I am breaking my Lough Derg fast on these, long before the appointed midnight hour[2] when my station will end; and on the wild raspberries that are as plentiful as blackberries in September. Sharp and sweet and here for the taking, all along the old hedge that slopes gradually to the shore of Lough Erne. And then on sheep's sorrel, its soft inner leaves chewy and tart as nasturtium.

The farm track turns abruptly to the right. I wade on through long seeding grass and meadow vetches. There is only a faint cleft of disturbance to show that anyone has been this way all summer. Hawthorn and blackthorn bushes almost hide what I am looking for, and when I find the slender hooped railing that encloses it, the grassheads reach almost to its top.

Caldragh is a circular graveyard, sloping, full of drifts of vegetation. It is scarcely clearer of long grass and willowherb than the meadow that runs all round it. The part nearest the lough is darkly overhung with trees. I enter through a gateway, walk in thirty paces or so to the centre, and there are the stone heads, carved pillars so grass-surrounded and unassuming I might have taken them for ordinary headstones at a distance, if I had not known about them. But their smallness takes me by surprise. The shorter of the two scarcely reaches my waist. Mossed and weathered slabs lean at odd angles around them. This place has been used as a graveyard down the Christian centuries, too, though the stone heads date from Ireland's pre-Christian past.

The bigger head, the Caldragh Idol, is Heaney's 'two-faced' stone. The wide-open eyes and parted lips yield nothing now of their ritual 'meaning', not after two millennia. They do indeed answer 'silence with silence'. But, seeing them in the stone flesh, I am unhappy about the negative feel of that epithet 'two-faced', for the two faces are not in some tricksy or hypocritical relationship, but lie clear and open like Janus's. Janus: spirit of the threshold, of inner and outer, of all beginnings.[3] Between them the faces take in opposite views, embrace the whole circle about them. Their silence matches the stillness of their balance. And at their physical centre is a hollow cavity, a sky-facing cavelet to hold a pool of rainwater – Heaney's 'stoup'. There is water there now, and I brush my fingers at its mossy edge, as if it were holy water in some roofless porch.

*   *   *

6 August

Narin.

I have made a great circuit north and then west round Donegal. My motion has been leftwise, against the direction of clocks and suns – and stations. Last night from the Bloody Foreland[4] of Ireland's north-western corner, I watched the sun go down into the Atlantic. Tory Island's harsh saw-tooth horizon was behind my right shoulder, to the north; to my left and the south, in paler and paler shimmers of grey, were Gola, Owey, Cruit, Aran, and a hundred other islands and near-islands. And beyond them, the unmistakeable stacks and sweet rearing up of the Glencolumbcille peninsula.

Glencolumbcille! There was no refusing the summons of that furthest filmy horizon. Once I saw it, I knew I must make for it, with as straight a Sweeney flight as the roads of the west would allow, and sleep that night under its shelter, close to the dunes of Narin and the safe harbour of Iniskeel.

So I wake now with the dunes in my eye, uncurl from the car, and walk into Narin on the landward side of the marram. I take my boots off and go barefoot again, no longer on the tonsured lawns and flagstones of Station Island, but slushing through the green grass and rushes at the edge of Narin's lake. Here the *machair* and the wetland meet and mingle imperceptibly. Sand and peat ooze up together between my toes, and marble my feet with their black and cream.

'You'll not get to the island for a day or two yet.' I'm standing on the tarmac roadway by Narin strand, asking a roadman with a shovel about the state of the tides. 'Not comfortably, anyway.' But later, an hour before low water, I am back on the strand. Once more I strip my feet bare.

I see Iniskeel at the end of a long vee of rippled sand, the bar built up by the meeting and withdrawing of the separated tidal flows. As I approach it along the sand, I feel as though I am walking to it on the seabed just like the

Israelites when they crossed the bed of the Red Sea, and that the Atlantic is reared up in patient walls to each side of me. The curvature of the earth seems dizzyingly apparent.

It is low water, but one last channel of sea has not withdrawn. Iniskeel is circled still by the salt waters, cross-pleating their surprised currents through rocks and weed. I walk in up to my thighs, my toes fingering cautiously through the weedy bits in case the spirits or descendents of those crabs I hooked in my childhood take their revenge. But it is not a difficult wading. It gets no deeper, and the channel is only slightly wider than, say, the Termon River.

I reach the island's small strand, and its deserted house, and walk on round to the half-fallen buildings of the monastery. Outside the roofless church, Iniskeel's hole-stone rests, an improvised altar now, laid across grey stone supports. It is one of the many holed stones found throughout Ireland. Their use in rituals to do with love and fertility has only recently fallen away. Couples would clasp hands through such holes at their betrothal; pregnant women would draw some of their clothing through when the time for their delivery drew near.[5]

Iniskeel is empty of humans now. The cattle driven over for the summer grazing gather in curiosity at the fence. There is the dark movement of a startled Irish hare, the flash of a wheatear. Little ringed plovers run in small scurry-parties over the strand.

When I walk off the island and back through the channel's fragment of the River of Ocean, it seems to have grown no wider or narrower, but once I am above the high tide mark, up on the pale dry sand of the Narin dunes half a mile away, I look back to see the lie of land and water. Iniskeel is unquestionably an island again.

*   *   *

7 August

So. I have my brief Sweeney-time, and I must return.
Enniskillen. Dublin. Holyhead and home.

But not refreshed. The images and affirmations of
Caldragh and Narin fade as I complete my leftwise circuit
by bus, back across Ireland's boggy midlands on my way
to the ferry. They can no longer hold my deeper distress at
bay.

It is the first time I will have returned from Ireland cast
down and troubled. My previous pilgrimages to the west
have been the essential other life that makes my sea-less
city existence in England's Midlands bearable. Now, not all
the barefoot rounds in wild Donegal can dismiss the
larger-scale images of waste and suppression that I hold in
my mind's eye from both Station Island itself and Heaney's
sequence. The strong sense of the feminine that drew me to
this difficult pilgrimage is seen so exclusively through male
consciousness – both Heaney's and the Church's – that it is
distorted beyond usability for me, but not, sadly, beyond
recognition.

How such a vision needs the silence of its women, and
their madonna smile! Where can I turn to hear a real
heterodoxy in this land? One that offers me a way of
respecting the female experience in Ireland, finding a value
in it that at this moment eludes me? For I have taken into
myself that distortion, taken too much to heart the pollution
and drought at Heaney's heartland and mine. The male
orthodoxy of Ireland has revealed itself to me as it never
has before, on my earlier sentimental and sheltered
journeys to the West.

Heaney's voice may be heterodox on the island's
Catholic terms, but it assumes a patriarchal men-only
version of the world with just the same easy
unconsciousness of difference as the island's priests do: it
is, after all, 'the norm' to be male. And what a weight of
male poets there is here! The handful of women who have
made their names in the past have been balladeers of

religious or nationalist sentiment – no nourishment there, not for our times. The women who publish now are thin on the ground, and close to me in age. In Ireland I have had to look to the male poets as forerunners. There is a strange but explicable lack of the foremothers Virginia Woolf recommended us to seek out.

So. I have followed Heaney's footprints, and found that on Station Island the steps don't fit. Will I now return to other parts of his work and find dissatisfactions there as well? Must the rereading of once-loved texts after I have stumbled, clumsily, half-aware, on to a new level of feminist consciousness always be an experience of disappointment and of loss?

For so much of my life I have read poetry and fiction as though I were a man! The study of literature and the canon of works deemed classics have been so heavily male – not just in Ireland – that I and many women have become honorary males of the mind when entering the field, just as in childhood we became honorary boys: climbing trees, making bows and arrows, and wearing our grubby and torn clothing with pride.

Does the shift in attention, my starting to hear the silences of women, inevitably mean a loss of sympathy with so much that I have been nourished by in the past? On the other hand, ideas that have only been ideas to me begin to take on flesh. Luce Irigaray's proposition, for instance, that male representations of women distance us from our psychic identities. 'We are, Irigaray says, alienated from our being through existing in language only as a negative, a "hole", and through the psychic processes, determined in part by language, whereby we acquire our identities as women. ... it is the repression of her meaning that makes his thought possible.'[6] Those unspeaking, unindividualised women of 'Station Island', those disembodied breasts of the ninth and the twelfth poems – how can I read of them *unquestioningly* from any perspective other than the male one that I have been trained in from childhood? As reader and as woman, I have no ground to stand on here. I, too, am an absence. Where I thought I was in the land of my heart.

I am close to a despair that is to do with both Irish society and myself. I even begin to wonder whether I will ever want to return to Ireland after this trip. For the internment on Station Island has told me harsh truths about my own identity. I see now that in my own choices and responses as a woman I. have been, and still am, far more conditioned by my Catholic childhood than I would have believed possible. I left the beliefs and practices of the Church nearly half my life ago, and thought that that was enough to get me clear of it. Yet I am still absolutely the creature of its particular and suffocating patriarchy: passive, guilt-ridden, and endlessly accommodating to the men in the world and in my life. Too much of the time I wear a smile just like that plaster Mary's.

What shakes my heart most is the returning fear that this new and raw understanding of myself sheds such awkward light on areas of difficulty in my life with Michael: our second-chance love that has been so sweet, but also, I see now (looking over a painful distance towards my adult home from my childhood's country) too full of *my* sacrifice – that immolation of self that I was so expertly trained in. How automatically, despite both our protestations of feminist intent, we have fallen into the old patterns of polarity. Do our heads and hearts have no control, then, over habits of response formed so assiduously in our childhood's culture? Is there no hope that there can be radical and lasting change in individuals? In many ways, with Michael I act more out of my conditioned past than I ever did in my marriage. It is a grim recognition.

*   *   *

As the evening ferry swings out of Dun Laoghaire on its way to Holyhead, I do not, as usual, stay up on deck to watch the last outlines of Ireland slip into sunset: Wicklow's Sugarloaf to the south, the Hill of Howth and Ireland's Eye to the north. This time I am not sad at all to be leaving. I only wish that the boat could stay for ever in the waters of Saint George's Channel, and never have to make landing on the coast of either of my countries.

NOTES

1. Still the common name in Ireland for carbonated soft drinks.
2. On the third day of the Station, the pilgrimage regulations about fasting – only one bread and water meal in the twenty-four-hour period – do not end until midnight, although the prescribed content of that one meal is less austere. The regulations apply no matter how long or arduous one's journey. Some pilgrims celebrate with a slap-up meal as the seventy-two hour Station ends. Sean O'Faolain's 'Lovers of the Lake' arrive in Salthill (just outside Galway City) at a quarter to midnight.

> These homing twelve o'clockers from Lough Derg are well known in every hotel all over the west of Ireland. Revelry is the reward of penance. The porter welcomed them as if they were heroes returned from a war. As he led them to their rooms he praised them, he sympathized with them, he patted them up and he patted them down, he assured them that the ritual grill was at that moment sizzling over the fire, he proffered them hot baths, and he told them where to discover the bar. 'Ye will discover it . . .' was his phrase. The wording was exact, for the bar's gaiety was muffled by dim lighting, drawn blinds, locked doors. (*The Heat of the Sun*, pp.41-2.)

3. And eponymous god of the first month of each new year: January.
4. A memory from childhood: Three Church of Ireland brothers, all in holy orders, are staying at the same guest house as us in north-west Donegal. My father asks them one evening at supper where they have spent the day. They hesitate. At last one of them says very quietly, 'We drove up to the, er, the er, er – *Foreland.*'
5. See E. Estyn Evans, *Irish Folk Ways*, p. 301 and his photograph

of Iniskeel's holestone 'altar' (Plate 15: 1).

6. *Feminism and Poetry* by Jan Montefiore, pp.142 and 148.

CHAPTER FIFTEEN

The Most Difficult Door

25–27 August 1988

> I would read these words to you,
> Like a ship coming in to harbour,
> As meaningless and full of meaning
> As the homeless flow of life
> From room to homesick room.

Medbh McGuckian, 'On Ballycastle Beach'

Wet sand print, after a photograph by Eileen Coxon

25 August 1988

Ireland again, and the North. Driving west across east Derry.

I head up and away from the north shores of Lough Neagh, leaving behind me the loughside apron of land that is busy these days with so many factories and haulage depots and gravel works scattered through its reedy fields. I'm driving fast up the long haul of the Glenshane Pass, waiting for my first glimpse of the Donegal hills that will soon rise up, in the distance, beyond Derry City. I have spent more than enough time in the shaded lanes behind Toome, and in the graveyard at Bellaghy, and gazing through fine rain at Church Island in Lough Beg. East Derry is not 'my' country. I want to be clear of it.

Westward lies Donegal and all its familiar and beloved Atlantic coast. I have had enough of remembering difficulty, and suppression, and the senseless deaths of the men of 'Station Island'; enough, too, of a secretive and flat freshwater landscape that holds no important memories from my own childhood. My heart lifts with the rising contours of Glenshane.

Near the top, I pull off into a wide layby –

> parked on a high road, listening
> to peewits and wind blowing round the car ...[1]

Then I'm out of the car, and facing back east. The day has blown itself clear into the long light of evening. I can see for miles: the patched central plain of Ulster, the great and the small loughs, Neagh and Beg, and, in a blue smudge of distance, the Antrim and Belfast hills. The sky is without haze. The low beams from the west sharpen the detail in a hundred fields.

As I watch, the chill of a storm cloud takes the sun from my back, and in a few moments I am hunched against the first stinging onslaught of hail. I watch the fore-edge of darkness rush down the hill before me and then flood slowly over the plain below, quenching the bright fields and the slate-blue strip of lough waters. The storm cloud relentlessly covers the whole landscape with its own texture, erases all detail, all particular light and dark. By the time it reaches the far side of Lough Neagh, the plain of mid-Ulster could be sea, or merely another part of the clouded sky.

Just as in August last year, I have only two days free of commitments. My first thought has been to spend them in Donegal, to sleep in the car, or in the pup tent; at any rate, out in the wild: somewhere I can wake up and see the ocean before me, and then walk some remote strand of Gweebarra Bay, say, or the Rosses.

Why did I stop here and look back like Lot's wife, and open myself to the possibility of second thoughts? For when I see the eastern half of Ulster rolled underneath the huge cloud that still buffets me with its cold gusts, and shows no sign of blowing past, it suddenly seems like sheer escapism to go to the wild places of stone, and water, and rushes shooting green; to a rural and peasant world that was never, in fact, *my* everyday world at all. I need to go home properly, and with no concealing blanket of snow this time, no comfort of companionship to ease me. 'Come home east. Forget the west.'² Reluctantly I get into the driving seat and turn the car to face the opposite way. For I know now that I, too, have to take the fish-cold and bony hand of the city – not Joyce's city, but that of my own childhood –that is offered to me across the clouded miles. Didn't I try going to the west last summer after my Station? I found then that I could not any more fall into step with the stone-age women of my dream.

Is it reluctance or a proper piety that keeps me so long on the road of this return? It takes me nearly both the two days just to reach Belfast! First I drive east and south to the Mourne Mountains, spend a night at their base, and lie for the whole of the next morning in the whin and bracken and heather of Slieve Donard. I approach the city slowly, coming down to it from more familiar mountains, over terrain that is far more known to me than Heaney's County Derry. More intimately known when I lived in Belfast, I realise with a shock of surprise, than the Donegal I chose to return to first. I thread my way north through the twists and turns and switchbacks of the 'basket of eggs' country of Co. Down.[3] At one remembered sharp corner on a country road the whitewashed warning on the huge boulder at the bend is still kept white: 'Prepare to meet thy God'.

Swinging out to the coast in search of a remembered strand, I pass a sign to Ballykinlar Camp. *Ballykinlar* – of course! I had not thought that Station Island would haunt me here, so far from the west. But it was in Co. Down, just under the loveliest mountain skyline I know, that the most extraordinary 'Station' in the history of Lough Derg was made. The prior of Lough Derg gave his blessing, the prison governor his bemused permission. And from the eleventh to the fifteenth of August 1921, two hundred and sixty-four political prisoners interned at Ballykinlar Camp fasted and processed, did the circuits of their 'Station', just as if they were on the blessed island itself. 1921 – exactly sixty years before the hunger-strike of Francis Hughes and the rest. When I read of it in a devout book on Lough Derg last summer, I did not place the Camp so close to home.[4]

Past Ballykinlar now, I try once more to find that childhood beach. But the great dunes of Tyrella, which run for miles 'where the mountains of Mourne sweep down to the sea', and its famous strand are acres now of dereliction. Here is a place where I cannot, for all my intentions, walk barefoot on sand, or on the marram-covered hills. Every step is an avoidance, even with shod feet, of rusted metal and shattered glass. Over by the empty car-park, three men are dismantling the last of the kiosks, its corrugated iron sheeting bitten to awkward lace by decades of salt-laden wind.

*   *   *

27 August 1988

Belfast without snow. And on my own. There is no time to
look up friends, even if I wanted to. And I have no
relatives here any more. I park the car as near the city
centre as I can,[5] and walk across the square through crowds
as anonymous and absorbed as those in Station Island's
lake-bound piazza. At the far end I keep on walking, out
from the centre but still within the city, walking south to
the house I grew up in.   As I re-greet each remembered
curve and turning off the main road, helicopters sweep ever
more frequently overhead. The road itself gradually chokes
with cars and buses coming up the side-roads from the
Lisburn Road to the west.

Opposite the turning that goes down to my old home, a
small mansion has become the headquarters of the 7/10th
Regiment (City of Belfast), the Ulster Defence Regiment. A
timber palisade thirty feet high conceals and protects it. A
look-out post like a medieval turret stands on the corner
where I learned how to cross the road as a child: my first
school, run by Dominican nuns in what used to be Louis
MacNeice's house, stands right next door to the regimental
headquarters. The lawns, where we used to strew flowers
in procession on the feast of Corpus Christi, run down the
side-road right under the shadow of that palisade.

I turn away from the patient queues of cars and buses,
only faintly curious as to why they are forming. For I can
see my house through the trees, its pale Victorian gable-end
rising up like the west face of a distant, tiny cathedral. And
I walk towards the random shards it will hold there of my
childhood, the present moment quite dismissed. That high
attic window near the apex of the roof – yes, I remember
standing at it with my father on the morning after the car
ferry *Princess Victoria* went down in sixty-foot seas on the
Stranraer-Larne crossing, with all hands and all passengers.
We had travelled on it only a few nights previously. 'This
is the height of the waves last night,' I remember my father
telling me in some distress, as he tried to make the disaster

comprehensible to a small child. 'Supposing we were at sea, they would reach right up to this sill.'

My house is empty. It's a student house now, unused through the long vacation. So I can walk right up to it, and look through every ground floor window, through the letter box, into the yard. I am hungry to see it, but brace myself for the hurts.

The hearths of my old home are not just cold, they have hardboard tacked over them. The plaster mouldings of its cornices are gap-toothed. Each room looks like a waiting-room. Or a boiler-room. The backyard is partly demolished, its bricks a rubble of red and the flaking whitewash of countless springtime fresh coats. There has been no whitewashing now for many springs. I sit on some of the rubble. It was in the yard that our hair was cut and clipped, that baskets of chips hissed into the spitting lard of the pan; here that the docking man cleavered the tails of a litter of springer puppies on a wooden block; here that my brother and his friends made explosive mixtures of weed-killer and sugar in old treacle tins. In those days bombs were kids' stuff, just 'fun' – though one boy, I remember, lost a finger and an eye. A mistake in the timing.

Suddenly, real explosions begin to go off in the distance, like quarry blasts. It's not until later in the afternoon that I discover the extent of the uproar: the small bombs that exploded simultaneously in several different places at one o'clock, the hijacked and burning vehicles, the attacks on RUC stations, the huge car-bomb found and defused in the city centre. Today – of course, that's what it's about! – is the date set for the extradition of the Maze escaper Robert Russell from the Republic to the North. Hundreds have gathered at the Border crossing points to intercept the handover party, but he has been lifted by helicopter from a point south of the Border direct to Lisburn Courthouse, and Republican areas of West Belfast are alight with anger and despair.

But, for the moment, I am sitting in the past and in Malone, Belfast's leafy 'legation quarter', cut off from any trouble there might be elsewhere in the city. I am no part of it, or of anything here. In Belfast *I* am the ghost, the unquiet shade stranded, like Heaney's men, in lack of acceptance and lack of understanding. A seventeen-year-old takes so little and so much into exile. I have never, I realise with a shock at the implications, been an adult here. My forced leaving of Belfast twenty-four years ago is an unfinished story. It snags me continually in its over-and-over-again stuck record of grief. How to go forward from that repetitive and finally uncreative nostalgia?

My returns to Ireland's west have been, I see now, those of a child running to its mother for simple consolation. I have sought there the landscape of my childhood's delight, and also a more subtle and spiritual comforting. Last summer's experience at Station Island has indeed pushed me, rude and unprepared, into Experience, and made me turn away in puzzlement from the 'mother' that I see now with adult eyes.

Was that, in a way, what Heaney was doing in his 'peasant pilgrimage'? And is that why he, too, left Station Island unsatisfied at the last? There is a sense in which exile, whether chosen or imposed, cuts one adrift from a ghost-life of continuation in one's first country. Hence, perhaps, all the fascination Heaney has with the men who chose different paths from his own, paths that kept them within that first land's circuit, even the priest who supposedly left it far further behind.

To stick in the elegiac mode can be as unfruitful a way of dealing with the past as nostalgia. I begin to sympathise more with Heaney the pilgrim's desperate kicking away from community to 'swim / out on [his] own' at the end of his sequence. It still offers me no usable pattern, but I'm beginning to see how to move from the elegy of exile and loss into a new travelling of my own. One day, not too far away, I want to come home properly, for a time at least, and live as an adult here. And get to know some of the women of this city who, by all accounts,[6] are far removed from the passive, silent or smiling figures of 'Station Island'.

I want to do more than a one-off pilgrimage, or an anguished Sweeney flight across townlands I can only perch in for a moment before taking flight again. Like Sweeney in the very last poem of Heaney's book,[7] 'I would migrate'. Migrate, yes – move on a straight line, but one that is conditioned by the cycles of the seasons, and holds the circle of return, and return, and return as an under-pattern: a Sweeney existence that can be lived at the hearth, and in the city, but be a moveable feast. How different, I think, to be migrant rather than emigrant.

It will soon be possible. I have asked Michael to move out in a few weeks: we are parting, we hope, as friends. My girls are nearly grown. In my chosen 'migrant solitude', I will have the space to make my circle wide in the midst of the ordinary. And the silence to begin a time of listening out for the masculine in myself, an attentiveness that is hampered in me, just for the moment, by the quick and incomplete answers of living so very closely with a man.

I have lived very close to a man's particular and powerful text, too, for two long years now. I am thirsty for the voices of women, for a complex and noisy chorus to counter those haunted fruitless woman-silences of both 'Station Island' and Station Island. I want to listen out 'until the long dumbfounded / spirit br[eaks] cover', and sweet water fills again 'the font of exhaustion'.[8] Or until sweet milk is poured once again into a heel-print made in a cowpat, as it was for mad Sweeney in the end.

It's Heaney, however, who has led me thus far:

> Give him his due, in the end
>
> he opened my path to a kingdom
> of such scope and neuter allegiance
> my emptiness reigns at its whim.[9]

*   *   *

When I make my way at last through the city centre
(Westlink is still closed, and this is my only possible route
north), past the crowds of shop and office workers
evacuated on to the pavements, past the cordons of white
tape that are the sign here of trouble, it is nearly time for
the ferry.

This time I am leaving from Larne on the Antrim coast.
All the talk on board at first is of the disturbances in
Belfast; but when the ferry swings out of the harbour, the
mood of the passengers settles. It is so warm that many of
us stay out on deck for the whole crossing. And the
evening is clear: so clear that, on this shortest of the Irish
sea crossings, I can see both countries, one on the west
horizon, one on the east, all the way across.

NOTES

1. Poem II, 'Station Island'.
2. Section 36, *Sweeney Astray*.
3. The affectionate local term for the drumlin areas of Co. Down.
4. Their chaplain had cleared it with the prior of Lough Derg,
and the bemused prison governor agreed to everything except the
all-night vigil. See Alice Curtayne, *Lough Derg*, p.101.

The name brings up another – and this time a family –
memory for me. Earlier in the war of Irish independence, in the
aftermath of the Easter Rising, my mother's first cousin was
interned here with several others from Co. Galway. A group of
them went on hunger-strike for better food and conditions. After
twenty-five days they achieved their purpose, but paid a long-
term price. For the rest of their lives they all suffered from
stomach troubles, except for one who already suffered from an
ulcer and was persuaded by the rest to drink milk as well as
water: his ulcer was cured! Several of these internees, including
my relative Paddy Beagan, went on to become members of the
Free State's first Dáil (parliament).

5. The central areas of most towns and both cities in the North

are restricted zones, where one cannot leave a vehicle unattended.
6. See *Only the Rivers Run Free* by Eileen Fairweather, Roisin McDonough and Melanie McFadyean, and *The Crack: A Belfast Year* by Sally Belfrage.
7. 'On the Road'.
8. Ibid. The poem ends:

> For my book of changes
> I would meditate
> that stone-faced vigil
>
> until the long dumbfounded
> spirit broke cover
> to raise a dust
> in the font of exhaustion.

That 'the long dumbfounded / spirit' is the silenced feminine voice in 'Station Island' is my own idiosyncratic understanding of the text.
9. 'The Cleric', from the 'SWEENEY REDIVIVUS' section of *Station Island*.

BIBLIOGRAPHY

AA Book of the Road, Automobile Association, London, 1950
ALLNUTT, Gillian, *Spitting the Pips Out*, Sheba Feminist
Publishers, London, 1981
BANCROFT, Anne, *Origins of the Sacred*, Routledge & Kegan Paul,
London, 1987
BELFRAGE, Sally, *The Crack: A Belfast Year*, André Deutsch,
London, 1987
BERESFORD, David, *Ten Men Dead: The story of the 1981 Irish
hunger strike*, Grafton Books, London, 1987
BLAKE, William, *Complete Writings*, Oxford University Press,
London, 1966
BRENAN, Gerald, *St John of the Cross: His Life and Poetry*,
Cambridge University Press, London, 1973
BRODY, Hugh, *Inishkillane: Change and Decline in the West of
Ireland*, 2nd edition, Jill Norman and Hobhouse, London,
1982
BUNYAN, John, *The Pilgrim's Progrss*
BYRON, Catherine, *Settlements*, Taxus, Durham, 1985
CARLETON, William, *Traits and Stories of the Irish Peasantry*, 1876
CARSON, Ciaran, review of *North* in *The Honest Ulsterman*, 50,
Winter 1975, pp.184–5
CLARKE, Austin, *Poems 1967–1974*, The Dolmen Press, Dublin,
1974
COLEGRAVE, Sukie, *The Spirit of the Valley: Androgyny and
Chinese Thought*, Virago, London, 1979
COLUM, Padraic, *The Poet's Circuits*, Oxford University Press,
London, 1960
CORCORAN, Neil, *Seamus Heaney*, Faber Student Guides, Faber &
Faber, London, 1986
CUNNINGHAM, John B., *Lough Derg: Legendary Pilgrimage*, R. & S.
Printers, Monaghan, 1984
CURTAYNE, Alice, *Lough Derg: St Patrick's Purgatory*, Graham &
Sons (Printers), Omagh, 1976
DALY, Mary, *Beyond God the Father: Towards a Philosophy of
Women's Liberation*, The Women's Press, London, 1986
DANTE ALIGHIERI, *The Divine Comedy*
DAVIS, Elizabeth Gould, *The First Sex*, Dent, London, 1973

DEVLIN, Polly, *All of Us There*, Pan Books, London, 1984
DICKINSON, Emily, *The Complete Poems*, ed. Thomas H. Johnson, Little, Brown and Company, Boston, 1957
Dream of the Rood, ed. Bruce Dickins and Alan S.C. Ross, Methuen, London, 1963
DUFFY, Joseph, *Lough Derg Guide*, St Patrick's Purgatory, Lough Derg, 1969
ELIOT, T.S., *Collected Poems*, Faber & Faber, London, 1963
EVANS, E. Estyn, *Irish Folk Ways*, Routledge & Kegan Paul, London, 1957
FAIRLEY, James, *An Irish Beast Book*, The Blackstaff Press, Belfast, 1975
FAIRWEATHER, Eileen, McDONOUGH, Roisin, & McFADYEAN, Melanie, *Only the Rivers Run Free: Northern Ireland: The Women's War*, Pluto Press, London, 1984
FEEHAN, John M., *Bobby Sands and the Tragedy of Northern Ireland*, The Mercier Press, Cork, 1983
FLYNN, Lawrence J., *Lough Derg*, The Irish Heritage Series No.54, [1987]
FRIEL, Brian, *Selected Plays*, Faber & Faber, London, 1984
GLASSIE, Henry, *Irish Folktales*, Penguin Books, Harmondsworth, 1987
GLOB, P.V. *The Bog People*, Paladin, London, 1971
GRIFFIN, Susan, *Made from This Earth: Selections from Her Writing, 1967–82*, The Women's Press, London, 1982
HAFFENDEN, John, *Viewpoints: Poets in Conversation*, Faber & Faber, London, 1981
HALL, Nor, *The Moon and the Virgin: Reflections on the Archetypal Feminine*, The Women's Press, London, 1980
HEANEY, Seamus, *Death of a Naturalist*, Faber & Faber, London, 1966
HEANEY, Seamus, *Door into the Dark*, Faber & Faber, London, 1969
HEANEY, Seamus, *Wintering Out*, Faber & Faber, London, 1972
HEANEY, Seamus, *North*, Faber & Faber, London, 1975
HEANEY, Seamus, *Fieldwork*, Faber & Faber, London, 1979
HEANEY, Seamus, *Preoccupations: Selected Prose 1968–1978*, Faber & Faber, London, 1980
HEANEY, Seamus, *Sweeney Astray*, Field Day, Derry, 1983
HEANEY, Seamus, *Station Island*, Faber & Faber, London, 1984
HIGHET, Gilbert, *Poets in a Landscape*, Pelican Books,

Harmondsworth, 1969

HOPKINS, G.M., *The Poems of Gerard Manley Hopkins*, Oxford University Press, Oxford, 1918

JAFFER, Frances, contributor to the Workshop Essay 'For the Etruscans: Sexual Difference and Artistic Production – The Debate over a Female Aesthetic' by Rachel Blau Plessis and Members of Workshop 9, in *The Future of Difference*, ed. Hester Eisenstein & Alice Jardine, Rutgers University Press, 1985

JOYCE, James, *Dubliners*, Jonathan Cape, London, 1944

JOYCE, James, *Portrait of the Artist as a Young Man*, Jonathan Cape, London, 1924

KAVANAGH, Patrick, *Collected Poems*, Martin Brian & O'Keefe, London, 1964

KAVANAGH, Patrick, *Lough Derg*, Martin Brian & O'Keefe, London, 1978

KENNELLY, Brendan, ed., *The Penguin Book of Irish Verse*, Penguin Books, Harmondsworth, 1970

KINSELLA, Thomas, *Downstream*, The Dolmen Press, Dublin, 1962; and 'Downstream II', in *The Penguin Book of Irish Verse* (see Kennelly above)

KINSELLA, Thomas – see Ó TUAMA below

LAING, R.D., *The Divided Self*, Pelican Books, Harmondsworth, 1965

LOCHHEAD, Liz, *Dreaming Frankenstein*, Polygon Books, Edinburgh, 1984

LONGLEY, Edna, *Poetry in the Wars*, Bloodaxe Books, Newcastle, 1986

McCAFFERTY, Nell, *The Best of Nell*, Attic Press, Dublin, 1984

McCAFFERTY, Nell, *A Woman to Blame*, Attic Press, Dublin, 1985

McGUCKIAN, Medbh, *On Ballycastle Beach*, Oxford University Press, London, 1988

MONTEFIORE, Jan, *Feminism and Poetry: Language, Experience, Identity in Women's Writing*, Pandora, London, 1987

Ó CROHAN, Tomás, *Island Cross-Talk: Pages from a Diary*, translated from the Irish by Tim Enright, Oxford University Press, London, 1986

O'FAOLAIN, Sean, *The Heat of the Sun: The Collected Short Stories Volume Two*, Penguin Books, Harmondsworth, 1983

O'MEARA, John J., translator, *The Voyage of St Brendan*, The Dolmen Press, Dublin, 1981

Ó TUAMA, Seán & KINSELLA, Thomas, eds., *Au Duanaire: Poems of the Dispossessed 1600–1900*, The Dolmen Press, Dublin, 1981

PAULIN, Tom, *Liberty Tree*, Faber & Faber, London, 1983

PHILLIPS, Tom, *Dante's Inferno*, Thames & Hudson, London, 1987

POWER, Patrick C., *Sex and Marriage in Ancient Ireland*, The Mercier Press, Cork, 1976

RILKE, Rainer Maria, *Selected Poems*, Penguin Books, Harmondsworth, 1964

ROBINSON, Tim, *Walking Out to Islands*, Lilliput Press Pamphlets No.1, Mullingar, 1984

ROBINSON, Tim, *Stones of Aran: Pilgrimage*, The Lilliput Press, Mullinger, in association with Wolfhound Press, Dublin, 1986

RUMENS, Carol, *Selected Poems*, Chatto & Windus, London, 1987

SEVERIN, Tim, *The Brendan Voyage*, Hutchinson, London, 1978

SHORTER, Bani, *An Image Darkly Forming: Women and Initiation*, Routledge & Kegan Paul, London, 1987

Sir Gawain and the Green Knight, ed. Norman Davis, 2nd edition, Oxford University Press, London, 1967

WARD, Margaret, *Unmanageable Revolutionaries*, Pluto Press, London, 1983

WARNER, Marina, *Alone of All Her Sex: The Myth and the Cult of the Virgin Mary*, Quartet Books, London, 1978

WATTS, Alan, *Nature, Man and Woman*, Vintage Books, New York, 1970

WATTS, Alan, *Cloud-Hidden, Whereabouts Unknown: A Mountain Journal*, Abacus, London, 1977

WELCH, Robert – contributor to *Irish Writers and the Theatre*, ed. Masuru Sekine, Irish Literary Studies 23, Colin Smythe, Gerrard's Cross, 1987

WILLIAMS, H.A., *The True Wilderness*, Pelican Books, Harmondsworth, 1968

YEATS, W.B., *Collected Plays*, 2nd edition, Macmillan, London, 1952

YEATS, W.B., *Collected Poems*, 2nd edition, Macmillan, London, 1963

The Pilgrimage Exercises
at Saint Patrick's Purgatory

The four pages that follow reproduce the leaflet that is
given to pilgrims when they arrive at Lough Derg.

SAINT PATRICK'S PURGATORY, LOUGH DERG

THE PILGRIMAGE EXERCISES

approved by + Joseph, Bishop of Clogher, 1986.

THE FAST

The pilgrim observes **a complete fast from all food and drink** (plain water excepted) from midnight prior to arriving on Lough Derg. The fast continues for three days during which one Lough Derg meal a day is allowed.

The first meal may be taken when the pilgrim has made at least one Station on the Island, the second at any time in the afternoon of the second day, and the third at any time on the third day after leaving Lough Derg.

The meal of the third day should be similar to those taken on the Island. On this day pilgrims may also drink mineral waters as often as they wish after departure. The fast ends at midnight of the third day.

THE VIGIL

The Vigil is the chief penitential exercise of the Pilgrimage and means depriving oneself of sleep, completely and continuously, for 24 hours. It begins at 10.00 p.m. on the first day and ends after Benediction on the second day. At that time the pilgrim retires to bed.

THE STATIONS

Having arrived on the Island the pilgrim goes to the hostel, removes all footwear and begins the first Station. Three Stations are completed before 9.20 p.m. All the prayers of these Stations are said silently.

A Station is fully described overleaf.

The prayers of four Stations are said aloud in common in the Basilica during the night of the Vigil. Between these Stations pilgrims may leave the Basilica, use the night shelter, and walk around the immediate vicinity of the Basilica only, taking care to keep their voices down.

A further Station is made outside in the morning after the Sacrament of Reconciliation and a final one on the third day after Mass.

Order of Station

NOTE—The *Creed* in the Station is the *Apostles' Creed* as on the next page.

Begin the Station with a visit to the Blessed Sacrament in **St. Patrick's Basilica.**

Then go to **St. Patrick's Cross,** near the Basilica; kneel, and say one *Our Father,* one *Hail Mary* and one *Creed.* Kiss the Cross.

Go to **St. Brigid's Cross,** on the outside wall of the Basilica; kneel, and say three *Our Fathers,* three *Hail Marys* and one *Creed.* Stand with your back to the Cross, and, with arms outstretched, renounce three times the World, the Flesh and the Devil.

Walk slowly, by your right hand, four times around **the Basilica,** while praying *silently* seven decades of the Rosary and one *Creed* at the end.

Go to the penitential cell or "bed" called **St. Brigid's Bed** (the one nearest to the bell-tower) but if there is a queue take care to join it before going to the Bed.

At the Bed
(a) walk three times around the outside, by your right hand, while saying three *Our Fathers,* three *Hail Marys* and one *Creed;*
(b) kneel at the entrance to the Bed and repeat these prayers;
(c) walk three times around the inside and say these prayers again;
(d) kneel at the Cross in the centre and say these prayers for the fourth time.

Repeat these exercises at
St. Brendan's Bed,
St. Catherine's Bed,
St. Columba's Bed.

Walk six times around the outside of **the large Penitential Bed** (which comprises St. Patrick's Bed and that of Ss. Davog and Molaise) while saying six *Our Fathers*, six *Hail Marys* and one *Creed*.

Kneel at the entrance to **St. Patrick's Bed** (nearer the men's hostel) and say three *Our Fathers*, three *Hail Marys* and one *Creed*. Walk three times around the inside while repeating these prayers. Kneel at the Cross in the centre and say them again.

Kneel at the entrance to **the Bed of Ss. Davog and Molaise** (nearer the water's edge) and say three *Our Fathers*, three *Hail Marys* and one *Creed*. Walk three times around the inside while repeating these prayers. Kneel at the Cross in the centre and say them again.

Go to **the water's edge;** stand, and say five *Our Fathers*, five *Hail Marys* and one *Creed*. Kneel and repeat these prayers.

Return to **St. Patrick's Cross;** kneel, and say one *Our Father*, one *Hail Mary* and one *Creed*.

Conclude the Station in **the Basilica** by saying five *Our Fathers*, five *Hail Marys* and one *Creed* for the Pope's intentions.

THE APOSTLES' CREED

I believe in God, the Father almighty, creator of heaven and earth.

I believe in Jesus Christ, his only Son, our Lord. He was conceived by the power of the Holy Spirit and born of the Virgin Mary. He suffered under Pontius Pilate, was crucified, died, and was buried. He descended to the dead. On the third day he rose again. He ascended into heaven, and is seated at the right hand of the Father. He will come again to judge the living and the dead.

I believe in the Holy Spirit, the holy catholic Church, the communion of saints, the forgiveness of sins, the resurrection of the body and the life everlasting.   Amen.

Order of Exercises

FIRST DAY

12.00 midnight–Begin fast.

Pilgrims arrive as early as possible (any day from June 1 to August 13), register and await boat.

Boats: 11.00 a.m. - 12.00 noon; 12.45 p.m. - 3.00 p.m.

11.00 a.m.–Begin Stations and complete three before 9.20 p.m.

6.30 p.m.–Evening Mass.

9.30 p.m.–Night Prayer and Benediction.

THE VIGIL

10.15 p.m.–Introduction to Vigil.

11.45 p.m.–Rosary.

12.30 a.m.–Fourth Station.

2.00 a.m.–Fifth Station.

3.30 a.m.–Sixth Station.

5.00 a.m.–Seventh Station.

6.30 a.m.–Morning Prayer and Mass.

8.45 a.m.–Sacrament of Reconciliation.

Afterwards make Eighth Station.

12.00 noon–Renewal of Baptismal Promises.

3.00 p.m.–Way of the Cross.

6.30 p.m.–Evening Mass.

9.30 p.m.–Night Prayer and Benediction.

10.00 p.m.–Retire to bed.

THIRD DAY

6.00 a.m.–Bell for rising.

6.30 a.m.–Morning Prayer and Mass.

After Papal Blessing make Ninth Station.

10.00 a.m.—Departure of boats.

Note : 1. Pilgrims come at their own risk, must be at least 14 years of age, free from illness or disability and from the need for a walking aid.

   2. They may not bring to the Island cameras, radios, musical instruments or articles to sell, distribute or for games.

Rt. Rev. Mgr. GERARD McSORLEY, Prior,
Pettigo, Co. Donegal.
Off-season Tel. 072-61518. On-season Tel. 072-61550.

AFTER-DEDICATION

To Mary Robinson
President of the Republic of Ireland

who in the nearly two years since her election
to a post hitherto held by elderly and conservative men
has shifted the perception and the symbolism
of the feminine in Ireland immeasurably

July 1992